Time Chunking
Work Smarter, Achieve Your Goals and Enjoy More Freedom

© **Copyright 2019 - All rights reserved.**

The contents of this book may not be reproduced, duplicated or transmitted without direct written permission from the author.

Under no circumstances will any legal responsibility or blame be held against the publisher for any reparation, damages, or monetary loss due to the information herein, either directly or indirectly.

Legal Notice:
This book is copyright protected. This is only for personal use. You cannot amend, distribute, sell, use, quote or paraphrase any part of the content within this book without the consent of the author.

Disclaimer Notice:
Please note the information contained within this document is for educational and entertainment purposes only. Every attempt has been made to provide accurate, up to date and complete, reliable information. No warranties of any kind are expressed or implied. Readers acknowledge that the author is not engaging in the rendering of legal, financial, medical or professional advice. The content of this book has been derived from various sources. Please consult a licensed professional before attempting any techniques outlined in this book.

By reading this document, the reader agrees that under no circumstances is the author responsible for any losses, direct or indirect, which are incurred as a result of the use of information contained within this document, including, but not limited to, — errors, omissions, or inaccuracies.

Table of Contents

Chapter 1 - Making More Time for What Really Matters to You
Chapter 2 - What Is Time Chunking?
Chapter 3 - Manage Your Life, Not a List
Chapter 4 - Start By Capturing
Chapter 5 – Creating Chunks
Chapter 6 – Allocating Your Time Better
Chapter 7 – Chunking Work vs. Play
Chapter 8—Other Time-Chunking Optimizers
Conclusion

Introduction

Today, more than ever, we live in a society that requires us to do more and more in the same amount of time – or even less! That's why it's crucial that we're able to make very strategic use of our time every day. We all get 24 hours a day and no technology will ever add more to that. But what we can do – hopefully with the aid of technology – is to find ways to get more things done for the same amount of time.

It is easy to find yourself wondering when you encounter someone who has 'more' time then you. How does that person manage to accomplish so much in a week, when you can barely keep up with the day-to-day demands? Where do they find the 'extra' time that is needed to make them successful, instead of just keeping up with life?

The reality is that we all have the same amount of time—the major difference is in the way that we use it. People who use their time well are not stressing over the little things or procrastinating because they are overwhelmed by the thought of meeting their day-to-day expectations. They are not nit-picking at different areas. Instead, they use the strategies available to them (and everyone) to help them excel in everything they do. These people are excelling not because they have more time, but because they use their time more wisely.

So, how do you manage your time better, so that you can find the time to do more like all those other people in your life? Time chunking. Time chunking is among the most popular life management tools in the world today. It's a way of working that can help you work much smarter and, in the process, get more things done. In your free time, you can enjoy the things that matter most.

If you look for time chunking online, you'll find a collection of resources from business websites, life coaches, and various other people who believe their method is best. This can be a messy process. Instead, we have done the research and created an all-inclusive guide to time chunking that you will be able to use to change your life. You will no longer feel pressured by the sheer weight of the world around you. Instead, you'll be able to create manageable chunks with your time.

Within the pages of this book is information on time chunking that will help you use it to make yourself even more productive and successful. By the end of the book, you'll be in an excellent position to start chunking your work time and start improving your personal productivity.

If you're ready, turn the page and start learning how to time-chunk for optimal personal productivity.

Chapter 1 - Making More Time for What Really Matters to You

With much introspection, you'll see that life offers us a myriad number of choices and variety and with them come an infinite number of opportunities and challenges. It can be quite easy to suffer from analysis paralysis with all the available choices life has to offer. Just think back to what you did on your last day off work. Did you find yourself waking up energized, ready to use the 'extra' time in your week in a productive way? Or did you find yourself stuck in bed that morning, dreading the tasks ahead of you and wondering this will be the weekend you find time to do the things that matter to you?

Yes, we all want to succeed but often, we are left wondering whether or not we're on the right path. We want to achieve work-life balance but because of the large number of conflicts there are in our lives, it can be simple to find ourselves using up so much energy in just one endeavor or area of our lives. Things like striving for perfectionism and spending time on things that don't really matter can also leave you scrambling to find the precious time for those things you want to achieve in life.

If this describes you, it means you're currently unaware of what's truly important or what matters to you. The major problem is that when you do not know what you want, your life takes a directionless path. It becomes almost impossible to reach for the things you want or achieve any kind of success. After all, if you do not have any goals, how can you possibly expect to feel successful when you complete something? In turn, this aimless wandering renders you unable to pursue those things that truly matter to you. Although this kind of situation isn't something that can put your life in jeopardy, it can jeopardize the quality of life you live. Just visualize the life you want to live in ten years—are you taking the steps now to achieve it? Or are you just letting your life unfold around you as it happens?

What Really Matters to You

To live a quality life, it's important to make time for what really matters to you. And guess what? You can't make time for something you're unaware exists! That's why the first step towards living life to the full is knowing what's truly important to you – the things that matter most. And here are some practical ways you can discover those things.

Who Are Most Important to You?

Obviously, we care about the people who are most important to us. But that doesn't mean we always express and act out such care to them. There are times that we can take our family, friends and officemates for granted. When this happens, it's not just them that can be affected – we can get affected, too.

When you list down the people that are most important in your life, you put yourself in a position to be cognizant about them more often. And, in the process, you can intentionally value them and prioritize your relationships with them.

It's our inherent nature to be social. As such, caring for the people you consider most important to you is one way to live life to the full. And the only way to know who these people are is to sit down and think about them.

When we lead busy lives, it can be all too easy to forget about the people who matter most. Our significant other might get the short-end of the stick when we get snappy at the end of a long day or a friend might be cancelled on because you 'didn't have the time'.

When you are not in that person's shoes, you may not realize how damaging it is to neglect someone. You often leave them feeling as if they do not matter in your life or that you have better things to do. Of course, this might not be the reality. But if you cancel plans too many times and stop reaching out, the people closest to you might just drift away.

What Do You Enjoy Doing Most?

Other people enjoy cross-stitching. Others enjoy trying out new foods at new restaurants. Others find immense joy in running outdoors or going on regular hikes in the woods or the boondocks. How about you – what do you enjoy doing the most?

Without a shadow of a doubt, things you enjoy doing most are some of the most important things in your life, i.e., they truly matter. They make you come alive and help you recharge from a long week at work. As with identifying the most important people in your life, identifying things that you love doing can help you make time for them because you can only make time for things you are aware exist.

If you are having trouble, think about it this way—what would you do if you had two whole weeks with no responsibilities? If your house stayed clean and your boss told you to take two weeks off, how would you spend your time? Close your eyes and visualize yourself feeling happy. What are you doing at that moment? Are you lying on a beach somewhere with the sand on your face and a book in your hand? Are you taking in the sights and sounds from a hike in the woods? Are you creating something like a piece of clothing or art?

One of the reasons that people lose sight of the things that they enjoy is because it has been a long time since they have genuinely enjoyed themselves. If you do not know what hobbies you enjoy, take some time to try something new! If money wasn't an object and you didn't have to consider your skill level, what would you do or create? Would you work on cars or perfect your fly-fishing technique? Would you teach yourself to bake or go snorkeling? The only limit to the activities that you try is what you are willing to do. Find those that interest you most and remember that you deserve to have some fun sometimes, too.

What Are You Good At?

Think about the talents, skills, and qualities that you possessed when you were younger. For example, were you good at spelling bees, baseball, math, or table tennis when you were a kid? During your teenage years, were you good at floral arrangements, cooking or solving mechanical problems?

What's this got to do with things that are truly important in your life? Well, there may be a strong link between those things and the things that you're good at. So, go ahead and think about them and list your answers down. Of course, you are not limited to those activities that you did when you were younger. Even though we might learn a lot about natural skill as children, people quickly evolve and realize that they have an opportunity to learn new skills, as well. Consider those skills you have practiced or learned through your life, whether through experience or a conscious effort to learn that skill.

Some people have trouble figuring out those things they are good at. Do not worry if you can't come up with anything on the spot. It can be especially tricky if you have a hard time with anxiety or a lack of self-esteem or confidence. People who do not believe in themselves often believe they cannot do anything right. However, this is not true. Everyone has one thing they are good at—and most have a lot more than that.

Remember that everything in your life is relevant. Even something as simple as showing kindness and empathy to people around you can be considered a skill. (It is even one that makes someone good management material). Remember that there is no limit to what you can consider a skill—if you are great at it, then own it!

What Were Your Greatest Accomplishments and Achievements?

Related to the things you're good at, you may also benefit much from thinking about and listing down your life's greatest successes. And by greatest, I don't necessarily mean grandest but significance to you in terms of how you felt or currently feel about them.

Do you feel excited about such achievements? Are you proud of your accomplishments? If you feel like that towards them, it means they give a great deal of satisfaction and joy, which is the primary characteristic of your greatest accomplishments. And they may also have a strong link to what you consider most important in your life.

For something to be considered a great achievement, it only has to be significant to you. Some students go through their entire school career without receiving any awards. Even if they were a good student, they might not have stood out. Keep in mind that someone else's recognition of your talents has no merit on their significance. What truly matters is that you recognize your own talents and abilities.

When you think of it, anything that you do has the possibility to be a significant achievement. For the average person, passing high school at age 21 might seem a little past the curve. For someone who became a teen parent, had a drug addiction, or struggled with their physical or mental health, however, graduating high school at 21 can be a grand accomplishment. It is significant in the way that it represents their dedication and their commitment to coming back and finishing the work.

What Do People Say Are Your Best Qualities?

While you can discover your strengths and great qualities through introspection, it's always a good idea to run them by those who know you well and ask them for what they think are your best qualities. For one, there will always be some sort of bias when it comes to identifying our best qualities, i.e., we may over-estimate the best and under-estimate the worst. By asking other people, you'll have the opportunity to receive objective feedback about your perceived best qualities and characteristics.

Another reason why it's always better to ask those closest to you for your best qualities is perspective. You may also be unaware of some of your best characteristics and qualities because of blind spots. By asking other people, you can enjoy the benefit of being able to discover those strengths of yours that lie within your blind spots.

If you are still having trouble, consider asking a friend or relative to help you list your skills. You do not have to tell them why you want to know your best qualities. If they ask and you are uncomfortable sharing, tell them you are practicing for a possible job promotion or that you are trying to create a resume.

By asking those who know you well, you may discover, among other things:

1. You have overflowing compassion towards poor people on the street;
2. You're a very good listener;
3. You give very good relationship advice;
4. You're the boss' go-to person whenever some sort of emergency or crisis hits the department; or
5. You're effortlessly good at selling ice to Eskimos and that you're one of the company's best salespeople.

Often times, what's most important to you is related to the things other people say you're really good at. For example, you may have learned how to be very good at giving relationship advice because your personal relationships are very important to you. As a result of such importance, you learned to look for ways to make your most important relationships (marriage, friendships, parents, etc.) joy-filled, intimate and satisfying. And the things you learned you're able to share with others who are experiencing relationship-related challenges, which they appreciate.

Mindsets for Pursuing What Matters in Your Life

More than just identifying what are the most important things in your life, you must also pursue those things. Otherwise, they won't be able to make a joyful and satisfying difference in your life. And there are important mindsets you must have to be able to successfully pursue such things.

<u>Difficult Doesn't Mean You Should Ditch Them</u>

One of the most unfortunate things in the world is people choosing not to pursue things that they've acknowledged to be important to them simply because they think doing so can be difficult, i.e., that they should ditch such pursuits simply because it's difficult. Many times, there's a direct correlation between difficulty and satisfaction of accomplishment, i.e., the more challenging something is, the greater the satisfaction one gets from accomplishing it.

I'm not saying that you shouldn't seriously consider the challenges of pursuing something that's very important to you and just go gung-ho blindly. No, that would be a foolish thing to do. For example, it wouldn't be wise to go on an around-the-world trip if you don't have the money for it, regardless of how important that is to you. Getting buried in personal debts won't make pursuing that trip worth it. What's worse, you may even end up stranded half-way around the world, without any family or friends nearby to support you or give you a hand.

On the other hand, it doesn't mean you should ditch it altogether. Just because you don't have the resources now shouldn't mean giving up on it altogether. For this, I submit to you the wisdom of two of my most favorite sayings:

> *"How do you eat an elephant? One bite at a time."*

> *"Rome wasn't built in a day but they were busy laying bricks every hour."*

In short, break down that ambitious goal into many smaller chunks spread across several months or years. While you may not necessarily be able to afford to go on that round-the-world trip now or in the next year or two, breaking that ambition down into smaller and achievable goal chunks can help you find more joy and satisfaction in your life along the way. And as you accomplish more and more of those smaller goal chunks, you'll find an increasing sense of excitement, joy and confidence welling up in you. And even with those alone, you can already start making your life much more productive because as you accomplish more of your smaller goals, the more motivated you'll become to do even better at work or business and get more things done.

Learning to set ambitious goals is the only way you will achieve the things you want in life. Think back to the last time you felt uncomfortable doing something. For example, you might have been uncomfortable sharing an idea at a business meeting or meeting your romantic interest's parents for the first time. However, when you do not take any risk, and you stay within your comfort zone, it makes doing the things you want impossible. You cannot possibly expect to stand out to your boss if you never speak up or do anything significant to set yourself apart from other people at your company. Likewise, you cannot expect to build a successful relationship with someone if you are too intimidated to meet their parents.

When you are faced with something that seems incredibly uncomfortable, take the time to prepare for it. Set small, related milestones that will help bring you closer to your goal. For example, you might practice doing a SWOT (strengths, weaknesses, opportunities, threats) analysis with ideas you have at home. This will help you quickly evaluate your own ideas before presenting them to the group. When you are confident in your idea, you'll be more confident in sharing it.

Humans are not meant to feel comfortable in life. Yes, being comfortable feels nice. There is stability and a lower likelihood of failure. However, the people who are most successful in life are not the ones stuck in dead-end jobs or relationships they are unhappy with. The people who are most successful are those who learn to embrace their discomfort and look at overcoming it as a challenge. Once they do overcome it, the discomfort often pays off in that area of their life as they achieve more and do better.

Pursuing the Important Things and Making Ends Meet Can Co-Exist

Related to the previous mindset, the idea that pursuing what's important in life will compromise one's ability to make ends meet isn't so accurate. Why? Not all of the most important things in life require substantial amounts of money. For example, continuous learning can be accomplished for less than $20 monthly! One of the best and most enjoyable ways to continuously learn is reading a new book every month, which isn't expensive when you consider the fact that some of the best new titles on Amazon.com's Kindle Store costing less than $20. That's $20 at most every month! How expensive is that?

And even then, not all of the things that you may find to be truly important in life require money! If you're a deeply religious person who finds it important to connect with your deity of choice, praying is one of the best ways you can do so without having to spend a dime. If you value spending quality time with your spouse regularly and staying in shape, you can take daily morning brisk walks together around your village or the park. And I'm sure you know that having sex with your spouse is one of the best and free ways to spend quality time together, right? Right!

The key to making ends meet and pursuing your goals is learning to invest in yourself. You do not have to invest money—but invest your time. When you have a goal, set out a clear set of steps to reach it. Climb each milestone as a small hurdle and eventually you'll be at the top of the tall mountain you have built for yourself, reaching your goal in no time. Never accept that you cannot do something. Instead, find a way to make your dreams a reality. There is always a way—you just have to be bold enough to pursue it.

It's OK If You Can't Always Pursue What's Important

Many people think, feel and act extremely. Often times, it's an all-or-nothing approach, i.e., either things are done perfectly or not at all. This kind of mindset can kill any person's chances of experiencing the joys and benefits of regularly engaging or doing what's important to them. Why?

As one of the greatest ice hockey players that ever played the game once said:

> *"You miss 100% of the shots you don't take."* – *Wayne Gretzky*

If you don't accept the reality that it may be impossible to be always pursuing what's important to you, you will either stop trying to pursue what's most important to you or not try at all. Of course your day is going to be filled with less-than-desirable tasks. Even if you decide that you want to work toward becoming a doctor or lawyer, you might still have to work your dead-end job while you apply for scholarships or save money for college. Everything in life is going to take time. Think of it this way—each day that you do not take a step toward your goals is a day longer that it will take to reach them. Therefore, it is important to keep moving toward your goals. Even on days that you cannot work toward the things you want most, be sure to keep moving forward the next day. Only you are responsible for your life's forward trajectory and failing to move forward only limits what you can achieve with the time you are alive on this planet.

Besides, it's the sense of limited ability and opportunities for non-stop or perfect pursuit of such things that often gives a person a great deal of satisfaction and joy during the times such pursuits are possible. Can you imagine eating your most favorite food in the world in every meal every day for one whole year? I thought so.

Don't let your inability to perfectly or always pursue those that are most important to you get in the way of you actually trying to do so. Nothing in life is perfect, and that includes you. So, it's ok. Instead of focusing on the areas where you have 'failed' or 'messed up', take the time to think about the things you have done right. When you do reflect on those times where you haven't quite reached a goal or had the desired outcome you wanted, think of it as an opportunity to learn more. For example, someone cooking Thanksgiving dinner for the first time might not know to pre-bake their pie, so the crust comes out soggy. The soggy crust does not mean the entire meal is ruined. Additionally, it is a lesson in baking, as you have the opportunity to make better pies the next time around.

Perfection Isn't a Requirement

Finally, pursuing things that are most important to you doesn't need perfection. Prioritizing your marriage doesn't mean it has to be perfect and that anything less won't work for you. You can have a great but imperfect marriage, seasoned with occasional disagreements and discord. The key there is to have significantly more "good" than "bad". Nobody's marriage is perfect. There will always be a glitch every once in a while.

If you value continuous learning, it doesn't mean you should always be reading a new non-fiction book every month. There may be months when you'll have to spend so much more time at work, especially if you're starting up a new department, business, or product line for your company. As soon as your schedule frees up, resume your regular reading habit. Picking up your reading after a break is a much better alternative to giving it up altogether.

This same principle can be applied to dieting and exercise. Imagine that someone was trying to lose weight. So far, they have successfully lost 25 pounds. They are proud of their efforts, but one day, they find out that one of their favorite relatives died. Later that week, the person they were dating breaks things off. This is a scenario that can be incredibly emotional and this person might give into their cravings and eat fast food or a tub of ice cream. However, the emotional binge-eating only happened one time. If the person becomes angry with themselves for 'messing up' their diet and gives up, then they lose some of the progress they have made in losing 25 pounds. Returning to their old habits might even cause them to gain back more weight than they had lost. It does not make sense to hinder your own progress just because of a setback—you are only pushing yourself farther from the finish line.

If you go for perfection, you will never accomplish it. And knowing you won't be able to accomplish it, you won't even try to pursue the things that are most important to you. Remember that when it comes to pursuing what's truly important to you, small somethings always trump big nothings.

Living Un-Plugged

There has never been such a time as now when filling in time with images, words, and noise has been so easy. It's so easy that for America's youth segment (8 to 18 years old), media consumption or usage tends to take up around 7 ½ hours of their daily 24. If you consider the fact that "multi-tasking" has become all the rage these days, you can make the case that this particular age group on average spends up to 10 ½ hours daily on content consumption and usage. That's more than half of their waking hours every day! It's only in today's day and age that the default mode for most people is to "connect" to a minimum of one form of media that's considered to be personalized. And because it's considered as "default," being disconnected even for just a brief period of time can cause anxiety and stress to a person who's been forced offline against his or her will.

If you want to maximize the benefits from your surrounding environment and your relationships, you'll need to understand that today, there are 2 very different ways to live life: wired and disconnected. Each of these 2 states provides varying degrees and kinds of possibilities for living life.

Let's talk about "wired" living first. It's very easy to identify the benefits of being wired or connected to the worldwide web: you have the ability to go far and wide all over the world and you have speed. Imagine, you can reference and research practically all of the knowledge mankind has gathered throughout the centuries in just a few minutes – even seconds! Being wired has given us seemingly God-like knowledge abilities and as we continue using these abilities, we become increasingly more proficient with using such abilities.

Now, let's talk about living "unplugged" or "disconnected" from devices. In this state, we are much freer to make decisions, think freely, do things on our own volition, and generally express ourselves without being concerned about being pre-empted. Why? It's because being disconnected can shield our hearts and minds from unnecessary distractions. Consider the fact that people like the best basketball player in the world today, LeBron James, disconnect from social media during the playoffs so he can really focus in mental energy and what matters and keep it from "leaking" because of the millions of people who comment on the things he does or says. In particular, being disconnected helps him guard his mind and heart from negative and critical comments and reports, which allows him to stay positive, encouraged, calm and focused.

Now, I'm not saying that being connected is an evil that you should avoid at all costs. No, that's not my point. Remember, I said that both have their own set of benefits. What I'm proposing to you is you intentionally go offline or disconnected on a regular basis. When you do this, you'll be able to make more time for what really matters. Later on, you'll discover why disconnecting is crucial to freeing up more time for what really counts and becoming optimally productive.

When it comes to entering a disconnected state, it doesn't mean you'll have to pack all your stuff and move to the boondocks! While it's a highly recommended that you take out of town vacations to places that are far from the hustle-and-bustle world you currently live in once in a while, making it your permanent way of life is really neither practical nor optimal. In fact, you can do it in the comfort of your own home on a daily basis without going anywhere. Simple morning rituals or habits such as not looking at your phone to check your social media or email as soon as you wake up and instead, doing something disconnectedly productive such as drinking a tall glass of room temperature water as soon as you get up and meditating mindfully for at least 10 minutes before doing anything else. Early mornings are best, especially when everybody else is still asleep, because not only can you enjoy time disconnected from electronic stimuli, but you can also enjoy time disconnected from social stimuli.

You can also do this just before you go to bed. You can impose a personal cut-off time for yourself in terms of online or electronic connectivity. You can use this time to gradually "land your mental plane" from the sky of a stimulated state to the airport runway of a mentally, physically and emotionally relaxed state.

When it comes to disconnecting from your electronic devices so you can have more time for what really matters, there aren't any cookie-cutter solutions that work for everyone. It's like a tailor-made suit, i.e., the best ones take into considerations your unique characteristics and dimensions. For some people, mindfulness meditation or regular yoga works best while for others, it's running outdoors every morning with no earphones on that provides a great opportunity to disconnect, take control of their minds and keep in control. For the spiritual-minded readers, reading and reflecting on the Bible, Torah or Quran passages daily helps them continue staying in touch with and aware of themselves, their spiritual states and their relationships with others. The key is to know yourself. What makes you tick and get ticked off? Based on such information, you can have a very good idea of what regular electronic disconnection method will work best for you.

Chapter 2 - What Is Time Chunking?

Regardless of whether you are an entrepreneur, an employee, a professional manager, a teacher, a student, a stay-at-home spouse, a freelancer, an artist, or a high-level corporate executive, there's no doubt that you do your best to try and get more things done in less time. In other words, you're constantly trying to figure out how you can become even more efficient and productive with your time. Everyone wants to achieve success and the only way that most people know how to do it is by doing more and trying harder.

But there's a limit to how much you can do within a specific period of time. At some point, the tempting proposition of multi-tasking starts to become a very attractive alternative, especially when you know you can't put in more time to get more things done. Multi-tasking seems to be a practical idea because instead of dealing with the work you have to do, you simply work overtime! But there's one issue with multi-tasking.

Multi-Tasking is Not Effective

Yes, you read that right. Multi-tasking doesn't work. Well, at least not in ways that really matter. Why?

Multi-tasking is a concept that was derived from very fast computer processors that were started being produced during the 1990s – i.e., the Pentium series of computer processors from Intel, Inc. Because of the technological advancements in computing technology that had been accomplished by that point in time, which continues up to this day, computers became more and more powerful in terms of performing tasks. In short, computers were able to finish tasks at speeds that were practically impossible to perceive.

Now here's the really interesting part that will burst your bubble. Computer processors really don't multi-task. They perform one task at a time only. But because of the hyper speed at which computer processors perform today, they're able to switch back from one task to another at such a fast speed that it appears to the human eye that a computer is performing several tasks at once. It's like a juggler who is juggling multiple balls in the air. To the naked eye, it appears the juggler's able to focus his attention on all the balls at once. But what he's actually doing is just rapidly shifting his attention and his hands from one ball to another. After throwing a ball in the air rapidly, he focuses his attention on the ball that is closest to falling down so he can catch it and quickly throw it up in the air. By rapidly shifting his hands and focusing on each ball, it appears as if he's focusing on all of them at the same time while the truth is, he isn't.

So, when you're working on a paper on your computer while you're downloading a large file in the background, your computer isn't really multi-tasking. It's just able to shuffle back and forth between your word processor and your downloading activity. This will also explain why the more programs or apps you keep open in your computer's background, the slower it becomes at executing tasks, sometimes to the point that it can hang.

So, if a computer really can't multitask, what makes you believe you can?

Now that you know multi-tasking isn't really possible and what really passes for it is actually called task-shifting, allow me to clarify something. Multi-tasking (I'm just using this term for easier recall and familiarity) isn't always a bad thing. In many instances, it can really help you get more things done. But there's a qualification: the tasks you should be "juggling" at the same time should be those that don't require deep mental focus for optimal accomplishment. In short, you should only sparingly use multitasking on tasks that are no-brainers. Examples of these include:

- Gargling while putting your socks on;
- Walking to your next meeting that's due to start in 3 minutes while munching on a sandwich for lunch; or
- Listening to a podcast while on your morning run in the park.

But for serious personal productivity, you can't afford to multi-task, especially on tasks that require deeply focused work, where the consequences of missing out on key details due to lack of attentional focus can be disastrous like mistakenly executing a "buy" order for a specific stock instead of a "sell" order. Or when you're writing a speech for your boss and you forget to include key details that can make or break his career. For tasks like these, your attention must be focused on one task alone at a time.

Given all the argument against multi-tasking, making it sound like it's the devil's child, then why are we naturally inclined to multi-tasking? Why the constant urge to do so? Well, the answer may lie in our Stone-Age ancestors.

Back in those days, practically any new information acquired by our Neanderthal ancestors can spell the difference between life and death. For example, a simple rustling in the bushes may mean there's a predatory animal creeping closer to pouncing on them. That's probably how the human brain evolved to always pay attention to any new piece of information or stimuli that comes its way.

However, that evolution failed to devolve as human societies progressed throughout history. Even when risks for being fair game to wild animals dropped significantly over time, the human brain continued hanging on to this habit. Worse, never has been a time in human history when people are faced with as much information stimuli as there is now. The human brain, unfortunately, isn't wired to handle the amount of sensory stimuli that the average person is exposed to these days, thanks largely to the Internet. This may even be a contributing factor in the anxiety that many people experience in their day-to-day lives—people's minds are so over-stimulated that they are constantly experiencing information overload. That's why multi-tasking is a habit that we should all nip in the bud. Computers, which were designed to streamline processes that would take the average human much longer, cannot even handle the processing power needed to multi-task. They execute one task at a time and you should, too. Otherwise, you may find your brain feeling 'stuck' like a tab that is having trouble loading because you have eight other tabs loading in the background and music playing.

Higher Chances of Errors

I don't want to bore you with statistical mumbo-jumbo on this one, so I'll just use a fairly intuitive illustration of how multi-tasking can lead to more errors (both in numbers and in terms of gravity of errors). Have you ever texted and driven at the same time? Have you ever been in an accident because of doing so? If not, then I'm sure you've already read or watched news stories of fatal traffic accidents happening because of a stupid driver who was trying to multi-task by texting and driving at high speeds.

Driving is a task that requires serious mental focus because if you become careless and unfocused, even for just a split second, it can spell the difference between the life of a child who will grow up into a healthy adult or one who will be buried by his or her parents in extreme anguish. But when you text while driving, your taking your eyes off the road and effectively, your hands off the wheel for extended periods of time. And if a child, an adult pedestrian, or another vehicle happens to cross your path during such extended periods of time when your attention is focused on your smartphone's screen, an accident is sure to happen.

While the consequences at work may not include destroying another vehicle or sending a person to the hospital ICU, making multi-tasking at work a habit can result in many errors that, when added up, can keep you from producing more in less time or worse, keeping the quality of your work poor, which can keep you from being promoted. Worse still, your poor quality of work may get you fired eventually.

The consequences of multi-tasking at home may not be as fatal to other people physically as when you text and drive, but it can be as fatal relationally to your loved ones if it defines how you spend time with your loved ones at home. Think about how upsetting it would be to go out with someone or make dinner for someone, only to have them stare at their phone the entire time. What if when you tried to talk to them, they shushed you so they could keep watching a video? Being inattentive can kill otherwise healthy relationships. So, if you want to keep the people that matter to you close, be sure to make them a priority in your life. This means avoiding taking business calls at dinner and refusing to answer emails when you are spending time with your significant other. Not only is it rude, but it is also incredibly harmful to your relationships!

So, focus! Don't be a scatterbrain.

It Takes Much Longer To Accomplish Tasks

Now that you know what you believe multi-tasking to be, it's time to take a look at another sinister reason why it's actually a personal productivity killer rather than a booster.

Shifting focus in and out of a task that requires deep focus isn't as simple as it seems. While it's not as complicated as stopping what you're doing to focus on something else and coming back to it after a few minutes and repeating the cycle all over again, the ability to hit the ground running again when you refocus isn't that easy to achieve. When you're working on something that requires deep focus and you allow your attention to go somewhere else, you break your mental momentum to build momentum on the new focus of your attention. When you decide to go back to the first task, you will then need to break the momentum of your new task, shift your focus and attention on the first or previous one, and attempt to build momentum again. So, when you "multi-task," i.e., attempt to juggle two things alternately within the same time frame, you'll end up not being able to build and sustain enough momentum to finish tasks at the soonest and most efficient time possible because you'll always have to stop and go.

Think of it this way. Let's say you have 2 routes you can take going from Point A to Point B, which are 100 miles apart. Route A is a freeway that has no intersections or humps, which allows you to put your pedal to the metal and drive your car as fast as you can for the whole trip. Route B will take you through the heart of 3 major cities during rush hours, which means you will be stopping and starting frequently. Between Routes A and B, which do you think will get you to Point B faster and with less gas consumption?

That's right: Route A because you can hit the highest gear and stay on cruise control all through the trip. Not only is it obviously much faster than driving through key cities during rush hours, but driving straight without any need to stop and go also allows you to use less gas because you'll be driving with optimal momentum at optimal speed without the need to keep changing gears. If you take Route B, you will have to stop frequently because of traffic, you won't be able to build and sustain mental momentum to get there faster and more accurately, and you will have to expend a whole lot more mental energy and willpower when you frequently have to start from a dead stop. Can you imagine having to mentally go back to the start every time you shift your focus and attention back and forth among tasks?

Multi-tasking is the mental equivalent of Route B. You'll frequently have to start mentally from scratch just to get up to speed again with what you were previously doing every time you have to refocus on the task at hand.

But to give you a more specific idea of how much longer it can take you to finish tasks when you juggle your focus from one to another when you multi-task, consider a study from the University of California Irvine. According to the study's leader Gloria Mark:

> "You have to completely shift your thinking, it takes you a while to get into it and it takes you a while to get back and remember where you were...We found about 82 percent of all interrupted work is resumed on the same day. But here's the bad news — <u>it takes an average of 23 minutes and 15 seconds to get back to the task</u>."

Think about it, it takes an average of about 23 minutes just to get back on track (mentally) with what you were previously doing. That means 23 minutes on average wasted because of multi-tasking. If you simply focused on doing one task at a time, you could finish your work at least 23 minutes earlier than if you multi-tasked. Now, can you truly say that multi-tasking is a personal productivity gift from God? If you were really honest with yourself, I'm sure you would now see that multi-tasking – particularly when it comes to tasks that require deep and complete focus – is from the pits of personal productivity hell.

If You're Smart and Want to Optimize Productivity, Don't Multi-Task

Multi-tasking has been scientifically proven to impair long-term personal productivity and cognitive performance. In particular, it appears that multi-tasking can impact a part of the brain that's crucial for career success. That's why if you're smart and want to really optimize your personal productivity, you should ditch the habit. It is better to ditch it sooner rather than later, too. You may find that breaking the habit is difficult, especially since humans typically follow similar patterns in their lives. It will take time to stop multi-tasking, but all the time that you earn back as a result is well worth it.

Researchers from Stanford University discovered something you probably know at this point already, i.e., that focusing on just one task at a time is much more productive than multi-tasking. In particular, said researchers found that people who are often exposed to multiple streams of electronic info aren't able to recall information, focus their attention on one thing and switch from one task to another as well as people who only focus on one task or material at a time. This is one way that multi-tasking can affect the brain, particularly in terms of cognitive performance.

What about people who seem to master the hack of multi-tasking? Surely, there may be exceptions to the rule, right? Well, those intelligent people from Stanford University sought to answer that, too. They grouped people according to the degrees by which they multi-task and believe that doing so maximizes their performance. What they found was interesting.

There was a great disconnect between the subjects' belief that multi-tasking helped them become optimally productive and their actual task performances. In particular, the researchers found that those who multi-task the most and supremely believe it optimizes their performance were the worst multi-taskers. They were worse than mono-taskers, i.e., people who focus on one task at a time, when it comes to personal productivity.

What was the reason for the very poor productivity of the subjects who multi-tasked the most? Impaired cognitive performance, i.e., poor organization of thoughts, inability to sift the irrelevant from the relevant pieces of information and slower task-switching speeds. This validates the principle that the human brain wasn't wired to focus on multiple things simultaneously and that multi-tasking – by going against this grain – significantly lessens a person's mental performance and personal productivity.

Another interesting thing why smart and productive people don't multi-task is that it reduces a person's intelligence quotient or IQ. A published study conducted by researchers from the University of London observed that the subjects who multi-tasked while performing cognitive tasks experienced similar declines in their IQ levels as those who smoked weed or were up all night. In particular, the men who participated in the study whose IQ levels went down by as much as 15 points due to multi-tasking effectively brought down their scores to the average of 8-year old kids.

But more than just impairing cognitive performance and personal productivity on a short-term or temporary basis, it appears that multi-tasking regularly can also have a long-term impact on both.

At the University of Sussex in the United Kingdom, researchers compared how much time people spent on using several electronic gadgets, e.g., watching a TV show while texting at the same time, to their brain scans. The researchers discovered that the multi-tasking subjects' brain density in the brain's region that's primarily responsible for empathy and emotional and cognitive control – the anterior cingulate cortex – was low. And low brain density can mean lower performance over the long-term.

While available studies haven't conclusively established which causes which, i.e., if brain damage leads to multi-tasking or vice-versa, what is established is that multi-tasking is related to brain issues and has negative side effects. And according to renowned neuroscientist Kep Kee Loh, who lead the University of Sussex study, it's crucial that people become more and more aware of the possibility that continually increasing use of modern electronic devices may be affecting our brains physiologically, which may be altering our cognitive performance.

Multi-Tasking and Emotional Intelligence

Let's face it: people who are multi-task during actual conversations are irritating at best. When they're on their smartphones or tablets while we're talking to them, they make us feel we're not important enough to warrant their full attention and worse, their gadgets are worthier of their attention than us. That's just plain rude and insensitive. Don't you agree?

It appears that people who tend to multi-task during social and personal interactions usually have low self-awareness and social awareness, both of which are crucial EQ skills for career and professional success. Premier EQ products and services provider TalentSmart found through testing over one million people for EQ that up to 90% of top performers they tested had high emotional intelligence.

So, think about it: if multi-tasking can negatively affect the brain's anterior cingulate cortex (an important brain area for emotional intelligence) as the study from the University of Sussex suggests, multi-tasking may result in lower EQ and ultimately, lower personal productivity and career success. In fact, some studies even show that emotional intelligence may be a better predictor of success than a person's intelligence quotient (IQ). Even though IQ determines a person's capacity for storing and utilizing information, a person's EQ greatly affects how they interact with people in their lives.

Think about some of the top management at your place of business. Generally, people who rise to the top are emotionally intelligent enough that they can manage problems with clients, employees, and business practices. They know when it is their best interest to be empathic or charming and when it is time to put their foot down and encourage an employee to do better.

People often say that the climb to the top can be lonely. While this might be true if you step on people on your way to the top, those with high emotional intelligence are better equipped to make and manage relationships on the way to the top. They associate themselves with people who are motivated and who can help them on their way to success, even if it is just with their influence or their motivational words. Being emotionally intelligent also adds a new element to the world of business, as it helps people get in the perspective of the people they work with.

Chunking – The Better Alternative

The human brain or memory is truly a wonderful and – dare I say it – miraculous – thing. It's more powerful than the most powerful computer every created. One of the ways it's so marvelous is how it's wired to utilize or manage memories. Chunking is a term that can help you get an idea of how efficient your mind utilizes and manages memories. In particular, this principle is a very important working concept to remember when you attempt to simultaneously work at completing several tasks.

So, what is chunking? According to Tony Robbins, who happens to be one of the staunchest proponents of this personal productivity concept, chunking refers to grouping information together into ideally-sized bits so that this can be used effectively and efficiently without being under great stress and being at risk of shutting down by being overwhelmed. Tony Robbins, being one of the busiest and most successful people in the world, uses chunking as a very effective tool to get his daily, weekly, and monthly schedules down to pat without dying from stress. Having taught this in his seminars, thousands of people the world over are using this as way to optimize their own personal productivity.

The key principle that makes chunking work is optimal management of information/tasks with minimal stress. When you really think about it, one of life's biggest stressors is feeling overwhelmed with too many things to do and so little time to get them done in. Chances are that your default mode when you start to feel more and more overwhelmed with the "backlog" of work is to organize the information on the things you need to accomplish by creating checklists. While it looks like a very logical way to manage things, so they can be organized and reduce mental fatigue, there's a point at which no amount of organizing can make a difference. In fact, if you have so much on your to-do list, it may backfire by giving you a very clear snapshot of just how deeply buried you are in work that you have to finish. So even before you start, you may already feel tired and overwhelmed.

Many people take an alternative approach, which is to break down a goal or major tasks into gazillions of tiny and more manageable tasks. For others, they take many of their similar goals and tasks and bundle them together. But just like to-do lists, these approaches can also backfire and lead to feeling overwhelmed.

If you feel overwhelmed with so many things to do that you feel like quitting or breaking down, what's the alternative? Well, one principle of chunking is that everybody – that includes you and I – can only focus on a limited number of things at any given point in time. On average, it appears that learning is best achieved by chunking information in groups of 3. More than that, most people tend to have a much harder time remembering or thinking about information. So, the ideal "chunking size" for information is 3.

If you find yourself unable to accomplish many of your goals, it can be tempting to think that you simply don't have the willpower and ability to do so. There's a pretty good chance that the reason for your inability to accomplish many of your goals may be due to the way you're chunking information. If you chunk correctly, i.e., take all the information that comes to you and chunk them in ideal sizes that can be easily managed by your mind, then you can put yourself in a much better position to achieve more success in life.

Chapter 3 - Manage Your Life, Not a List

Whether it's at work or at home, how often do you feel disorganized and overwhelmed? Everybody struggles when it comes to managing their personal and productive time and one of the most cliché statements in the world – one that most people use as an excuse or a crutch for inefficiency and low personal productivity - is supposed lack of time. But everybody gets 24 hours every day and if time was really lacking, how come many of the world's most successful people get so many things done in the same 24 hours daily? In most cases, it's not really a lack of time but poor time management.

Here's where it gets very interesting. Most people attempt to create or free up more time by organizing everything they need to do on a to-do list. They feel that being more organized means they can get more things done. But if that was the case, then why do millions of people have a very negative impression or opinion of to-do lists and why do people who do maintain updated to-do lists continue feeling overwhelmed and stressed at work or at home?

As mentioned in the previous chapter, one reason is that to-do lists themselves aren't the solution. Yes, they can help you organize the things you need to do or accomplish, but the human mind can only handle so much information or so many tasks at a time. Even the best organized to-do list can backfire if it's populated with so many "to-do" items that merely looking at them can make a person feel tired and overwhelmed at the start of the day! Can you imagine yourself staring at a to-do list of 100 items on a Monday morning? How do you think that will make you feel about the brand-new working week? It certainly is not encouraging.

Look, I'm not saying that to-do lists don't work. They can, if you will use them properly and not rely on them too much. But if you don't use them well, they'll just end up becoming huge stones that you can hit yourself over the head with. That's why instead of managing your lists, you should use your to-do lists to manage your life instead.

The Good and the Bad of To-Do Lists

Aside from having so much unorganized information on to-do lists, some of the other reasons why they usually fail to help get things done include:

- Comingling of personal and work items, which can create a deep sense of confusion;
- The items on the list aren't prioritized; and
- The list of items continues to grow instead of being reduced (more are added while less are completed).

But if you can manage your to-do list well, here are some of the benefits you can enjoy on a regular basis:

- You will always have a very clear idea of the things you have already accomplished as well as those that you still need to finish. Mark them as you go.
- Much less stress and mental anxiety because there's a great sense of freedom and relief knowing you've already put down on paper the things you need to do. The reason for this is by putting them down on a list already, you don't have to constantly worry about having to make sure you remember to do them when you need to;
- The ability to easily and effectively prioritize the things you need to do;

- You minimize the risk of forgetting to do something;
- You gain a greater sense of being organized;
- Much better ability to plan your days and weeks ahead;

The List is Your Tool, Not Your Master

You may think that this is a no-brainer, but here's the thing. Many people get subtly swept under the control of their own to-do lists without them knowing it. Why? It's because they're not cognizant enough of when they're becoming too focused and obsessed on the to-do list instead of the purpose for which it was created.

You see, people can get so obsessed with clearing their to-do list that it becomes all about checking off items on the list instead of managing the overall quality of their lives. For example, it can be very unsettling for a person who is so obsessed with to-do lists to make sure that all of his items for the day are checked off before enjoying the night with his family to the point that he will refuse to spend time with his wife and kids at night until he's able to check off the last item on his list. This happens even if the remaining items can be finished off tomorrow. This is an example of a person who is more obsessed with managing his to-do list rather than his life. He has lost sight of the fact that the list is merely a tool that is supposed to help him make time for the things that really matter like family.

So, before we get to practical ways to optimize your to-do list, always take the time to disconnect (Chapter 1) and reflect on your life, which includes, among other things, if you're in control of your to-do list or whether it's in control of you. In other words, are you managing your to-do list more than your quality of life or is it the other way around?

General Strategies for Optimizing Your To-Do List

Ok, now that I've clarified that the to-do list is a tool to enhance the quality of your life and not to hold you back from enjoying yourself, here are some general ways in which you can optimize your own personal list.

The first way is to categorize the information you capture about the things you need to do. Why is this an important first step? It's because studies have established that the human brain tends to be overwhelmed in the face of too many options, e.g., around 7 or more options. When faced with such, the tendency is to just shut down. It's for this reason that you should actually have several to-do lists or categories under which to classify or chunk information. For each category or list, do not go beyond 8 items. Examples of categories include "future projects", "for following up", "urgent", etc. There are no cut-and-dried labels, and these may vary depending on your personality and your actual responsibilities. However, a great resource for coming up with effective and manageable labels or categories is David Allen's book Getting Things Done, in case you want a very clear guide or ideas on the labels that may work for you.

The next thing you should do when it comes to managing your lists is to get a reasonable estimate of how much time you'll need to successfully complete specific tasks in your list. The task items in your list will each take different amounts of time to finish, e.g., some will take as little as 30 minutes only while other items may require several hours to complete. It's important that you can easily determine just by looking at the items on your to do list how much time you'll most probably need to compete them, so you can plan your entire day or week accordingly. Otherwise, you can easily screw up your day or week when you find tasks overlapping because of failure to properly estimate the time needed to complete them.

When making your to-do list, add another column to the list to indicate a realistic estimate of how much time you may need to finish the tasks. And more importantly, keep in mind the word "realistic." An unrealistic time frame can put too much pressure on you. If you're not sure if you have over or underestimated the required time, better to err on the side of caution and overestimate, i.e., estimate more time needed.

The next step to organizing and maintaining your to-do list is to prioritize the list of items on your to-do list. By this, I mean you will have to rank them according priority, sequence, and amount of time needed to complete them. To do this, add another column in your list to account for the order of priority. Then, categorize your tasks according to these 4 groups:

- Important and urgent;
- Not urgent but important;
- Not important but urgent; and
- Not important or urgent.

Tasks that you should put the most premium on are those that are important and urgent, obviously. But as the late, great Stephen Covey of the 7 habits fame taught, do your best to make sure that your to-do lists are mostly populated with important things that aren't urgent. Why?

Important things that aren't urgent will hardly stress you out and can contribute the most to your long-term success and life happiness. By virtue of being important, they will contribute a lot to your overall quality of life, but by not being urgent at the time you're already working on them, you don't have to feel like you always have to rush or are always putting out fires. Important but urgent things, on the other hand, are the single biggest sources of chronic stress because not only are they important, but you can't afford to avoid them!

Next, you must regularly review your to-do list, so it can continue functioning as a great life-management tool for you. A to-do list isn't simply about listing things you'll need to do. That'd be pointless if it wasn't used to make your life generally better.

So, do you continuously review your to-do list, so it can continue helping you make the most out of your opportunities and your life? One way is to review your to-do list at the end of every work week to see what else is pending and what you've already accomplished. Then update it with new things you'll need to do for the next week and use the updated information to plan your week accordingly. During your weekly to-do list review, choose which tasks to prioritize based on priority, time and sequence before plotting them on your schedule or calendar.

A good principle to live by when making your schedule is to never schedule more than ¾ or 75% of your available time. Why? If you book more than 75% of your available time, you will end up having too much to do, too little time, and too much stress, especially when curve balls and delays hit. By scheduling 75% max of your time only, you give yourself enough leeway for unexpected developments and time to enjoy life too.

As you go about your day, you should make an effort to do the most important things first. There will always be things on your to-do list that take higher priority than others. While these must-do items are sometimes more difficult, you should still get them finished as soon as you can in the day. When you do the important things first, you'll find that you do not have to scramble as much to get everything else done. Additionally, by doing the most important things first, you won't have to beat yourself up if you do not finish the ambitious list you have created for yourself that day. You'll find there are almost always things that can wait, especially if they are not activities that will contribute to the quality or enjoyment of your life.

Finally, don't beat yourself up when you cannot finish everything that you have put on your to-do list. As you learn how to better chunk your time, you will also learn that it can be challenging to separate your time accordingly at first. Something that can help a lot is keeping a journal. Write down your time chunks and mark off those activities that you do accomplish. Then, take a look at what you were unable to do. Look at the column where you wrote down the expected time for each activity and make a note of which areas you need to adjust. For example, it may take you 45 minutes instead of 20 minutes to check emails some mornings. As you discover the areas where you need more time, give it to yourself.

Do not worry if you are unsure of how much time you need each day. As you begin time chunking, you will become more aware of the amount of time you spend doing each activity in your day. You might even be surprised to find that you are spending a lot more time on certain activities than you expected. If these areas can be optimized, you end up freeing up time that you can use to do the things that matter.

Highly-Recommended To-Do-List Apps

One of the best ways to use to-do lists optimally to manage your life instead of focusing too much effort and time on managing your to-do lists is using apps. Here are some of the best and most popular apps you can use to efficiently and easily manage your to-do list so it doesn't get in the way of what matter most: your life!

<u>Wunderlist</u>

This personal productivity app has a user-friendly and clean interface that can make navigating the app intuitively easy. With Wunderlist, you can add and check off items in your task list, create sub-lists and set due dates and tasks for each task.

You can also create different folders through which you can segregate your tasks into specific categories. You can also filter your tasks and be on top of your schedule using Wunderlist.

Even better, you can create shared to-do lists with other people, e.g., colleagues, family, and friends. This can prove to be very useful for tasks that require collaboration with other people. The people to whom you share certain tasks or task lists can check off items once completed, which can inform other collaborators that those tasks were already completed.

Some of the primary features of Wunderlist include the ability to:

1. Make folders and lists;
2. Share tasks and lists;
3. Comment and note on tasks;
4. Use the app on any device, e.g., computers (Windows or Mac) and smartphones (Android or iOS);
5. Set task reminders and alerts; and
6. To easily import files to the app.

You can use the basic version of Wunderlist for free or Wunderlist Pro for $49.99 annually or $4.99 monthly.

Google Keep

While Google Keep may only have basic features and functionalities, it can be the appropriate app for you if you're the type of person who wants to keep your to-do lists very simple. Google Keep is mainly used to create and manage quick task lists that can be easily managed using any electronic device. It's basically a basic note-taking app on which you can write all of the important things you need to do, take pictures, record voice notes (if you can't or don't want to type) and check off finished tasks. And because Google Keep's connected to your Google Drive, it's very easy to sync multiple electronic devices on which you want to use it.

Some of the key features of Google Keep include the ability to:

1. Easily and quickly add tasks;
2. Set reminders for every task;
3. Collaborate with others on specific tasks via sharing of task lists;
4. Archive your notes;
5. Record notes from uploaded pictures or images;
6. Arrange notes in a list or grid view;
7. Organize notes using customized labels;
8. Prioritize certain tasks by pinning them on top of your lists; and
9. Record audio notes.

You can use Google Keep for free. There are no paid versions of the app.

<u>Evernote</u>

Evernote is a complete tool for taking notes that has features that can help you easily manage your tasks. Evernote also has a web-clipping feature that lets you save any online content or website to your Evernote account. You can use Evernote to share specific tasks or projects to other people for collaborative work. You can also integrate it with other work collaboration apps like Slack.

Some of Evernote's key features include the ability to:

1. Manage tasks and projects;
2. Use built-in note templates;
3. Access your tasks offline;
4. Drag and drop items in your task lists;
5. Use workspaces for tasks that involve several teams;
6. Use a web-clipping feature for adding online content or websites to your Evernote account;
7. Scan documents;
8. Integrate with other work-collaboration apps like Slack;
9. Synchronize with your email account;
10. Attach documents with notes; and
11. Use advanced searching filters.

You can use Evernote basic for free, Evernote Premium for $7.99 monthly and Evernote Business for $14.00 monthly.

nTask

This is a very good task management app that you can use individually or with a team. It has a simple and user-friendly user interface that lets you easily navigate through the app and use its powerful features intuitively.

With nTask, you can make tasks and sub-tasks as well as schedule them as one-time or recurring. You can also create projects that are made up of multiple smaller tasks. And more than just being able to list down the things you need to do every day, you can also organize, monitor and prioritize your to-do lists.

Compared to the other apps, nTask is more advanced. If you're the type who would like to have access to task progress reports, Gantt Charts (whoa!) and timelines for monitoring your projects efficiently, nTask may just be what the personal productivity doctor will prescribe for you!

Some of the app's key features include the ability to:

1. Easily and intuitively navigate through the app's powerful features via a user-friendly and intuitive user interface;
2. Create, organize, prioritize, assign and share your tasks;
3. Schedule your tasks as one-offs or recurring tasks;
4. Create stand-alone tasks or assign them under projects;
5. Create tasks using comments through a 3rd party app like Slack;
6. Assign a status for a task from a list of statuses;
7. Create tasks reminders, notifications and alerts for tasks and projects for your work teams;
8. Ensure a high level of security for your account using a two-factor authentication system;
9. Use workspaces specifically assigned to various work teams for simultaneous monitoring and management; and
10. Use the app on either iOS or Android phones.

You can use the basic version of nTask for free. If you want the full-features, you can subscribe to the nTask Pro plan for $2.00 monthly.

Todoist

Over the years, Todoist has become one of the most popular personal productivity apps and evolved to include more advanced features. With Todoist, you can also create, arrange and rank tasks as well create other stuff like sub-tasks, dependencies, projects and sub-projects.

You can also label your tasks and color-code them for easier organization. As with the other to-do apps, you can set due dates for your tasks. However, one thing that this app has that others don't is an AI-powered tool called Smart Schedule, which provides suggestions for when you can optimally schedule and reschedule certain tasks.

Some of Todoist's key features include the ability to:

1. Create and label one-time or recurring tasks;
2. Create tasks from emails;
3. Comment on tasks;
4. Set priority levels of your tasks;
5. Use built-in project templates;
6. Share projects with others for collaboration purposes;
7. Set reminders notifications via email and SMS;
8. Integrate multiple contact lists;
9. Back up your tasks automatically;
10. Customize your task filters; and
11. Synchronize your account across multiple devices on a real-time basis.

You can use Todoist's basic version for free. If you want to use all of its key features, you'll need to subscribe to their Premium plan at $29 annually.

Microsoft To-Do

This app was developed by the same team that created Wunderlist. Microsoft To-Do (MTD for brevity) isn't just cloud-based but it also integrates with Microsoft Office 365. MTD allows you to create tasks from zero or import them from other apps like Outlook or Wunderlist, which can be very useful when you need to continue working on pending tasks and you don't want to rewrite the whole to-do list. You can also customize the way your task lists are presented using different colors and themes, prioritize and arrange your tasks, and set reminders to ensure you don't miss out on any tasks.

MTD also allows you to practically eliminate confusion when it comes to your daily tasks and effectively streamline them on a daily basis. It has a feature called My Day list that lets you easily see the things you need to do for the day.

Some of MTD's key features include the ability to:

1. Manage your tasks well;
2. Create reminders for your tasks;
3. Set deadlines for your tasks;
4. Monitor tasks on a daily basis using the My Day list;
5. Prioritize your tasks;
6. Integrate your tasks with Microsoft Outlook;
7. Sync your MTD data across multiple electronic devices;
8. Create multiple lists;
9. Track your tasks' due dates to minimize risks of forgetting to work on them;
10. Share your lists with other people;
11. Use customized task list colors and themes; and
12. Use the app on both iOS and Android platforms.

You can use MTD completely for free.

Habitica

If you love playing video games, then Habitica may be your best bet for a to-do app. Why? It's unique in the sense that it transforms your daily tasks into a game where you can earn rewards. Because it adds an element of fun into accomplishing the tasks in your list, it may give you more urgency and motivation to finish your tasks on time or earlier than scheduled. Now, how cool is that?

With Habitica, you can make your own character, earn rewards and buy gaming-related paraphernalia like armors – all while completing the tasks in your to-do list. But as with all video games, failure to accomplish or tick tasks in your lists off can result in your online persona's deterioration and halt your progress.

If you're looking for a to-do app with advanced features, Habitica might not be the app for you. It's because it only has basic features apart from the gaming-related ones. Some of Habitica's key features include the ability to:

1. Segregate and filter tasks using tags and due dates;
2. Earn rewards for accomplishing tasks on time;
3. Create a highly-customized gaming avatar;
4. Use and monitor levels to track your task completion progress;
5. Create task reminders;
6. Chat with other online Habitica users; and
7. Complete customized challenges versus other Habitica users.

You can use Habitica for free.

Any.do

This is one of the easiest to-do apps to use for creating and managing your daily tasks. Any.do is comprised of simple folders for tasks and sub-tasks that can help you quickly and easily create new tasks and tick off finished tasks. It also allows you to easily transfer files using drag-and-drop.

One of the things that makes Any.do unique is the ability to input tasks using dictation. If you're on the go and can't afford to type a newly thought-of task into your app, you can simply speak your task into the app. It's like having your own secretary transcribing your instructions into your to-do lists.

Lastly, Any.do features a very simple user interface that lets you understand and easily use the app.

Some of Any.do's key features include the ability to:

1. Easily create lists and tasks;
2. Add new tasks to your list through dictation or voice;
3. Segregate tasks according to deadlines;
4. Easily share your lists with other people for online collaboration;
5. Easily set reminders and deadlines for your tasks;
6. Focus only on the day's tasks;

7. Organize and prioritize tasks through a color-coding system;
8. Set tasks as one-time or recurring;
9. Attach an unlimited number of files;
10. Create notes inside tasks; and
11. Use customized themes.

You can use Any.do's basic features for free. If you want the complete features, go for the Premium plan at $2.99 monthly.

TeuxDeux

Pronounced as "to-do", is a very visual to-do list app making it the "most beautiful" to-do app in the world, according to many people. Because it's very visual, you can easily see what you need to do for the day, create your to-do lists, and re-arrange them on the app's calendar. If you're the visual type, this may be the to-do app for you.

With TeuxDeux, you can write down your tasks anywhere. Later on, you can drag and drop them into your lists. If you weren't able to finish a task on the day it was supposed to be finished, the app will automatically carry it over to the following day's list. And you can schedule your tasks as one-time or recurring, too.

Some of the apps key features include the ability to:

1. Make customized task lists;
2. Schedule tasks as one-time or recurring;
3. Link tasks to other resources;
4. Switch tasks between your lists;
5. Automatically forward un-finished tasks to the next day's list;
6. Synchronize your task lists with your calendar;
7. Use the Markdown app for additional text formatting;
8. Sync your account on numerous electronic devices; and

9. Share with up to 5 other family members.

Unfortunately, TeuxDeux is only available on iOS devices. You can use the app for free for a limited trial period only, after which you'll have to pay $3.00 monthly to use it.

Toodledo

This to-do app concentrates on task management and as such, it allows you to arrange the tasks in your to-do lists in the easiest and simplest ways possible. You can add sub-tasks, notes, and priority level with every task.

Toodledo also helps you create outlines to help you better manage your tasks. Through outlines, you can display all your tasks and sub-tasks according to customized sections, which can help you get good overview of your tasks that are arranged accordingly.

Some of the app's key features include the ability to:

1. Create and manage tasks and sub-tasks, including folders;
2. Share your to-do lists privately and publicly;
3. Schedule tasks as one-time or recurring;
4. Write down quick notes;
5. Track and monitor habits;
6. Outline your tasks;
7. Write notes within tasks;
8. Schedule your tasks and create location-based reminders for them;
9. Integrate your account with 3rd party apps;
10. Create customized tags for organizing the items in your task lists; and
11. Use the app on iOS and Android smartphones.

You can use Toodledo's basic version for free, it's Silver version for $59.88 annually, and its Gold version for $89.88 annually.

TickTick

TickTick comes with a neat-looking user interface, which makes it organized, clutter-free and generally easy to use. You can create tasks, sub-tasks, create reminders and deadlines, and you can share your tasks and lists with other people. You can also schedule your tasks as one-time or recurring, too.

Some of TickTick's key features include the ability to

1. Create personalized task lists;
2. Set deadlines and reminders for tasks;
3. Schedule tasks as one-time or recurring;
4. Look at your tasks using a calendar view;
5. Set due dates by dragging and dropping tasks in the calendar's date boxes;
6. Share your task lists to other people for collaboration;
7. Set your tasks' priority levels;
8. Personalize your themes;
9. Create or input new tasks using dictation or voice;
10. Classify tasks using tags;
11. Track your tasks' timelines;
12. Evaluate your projects' progress using project statistics; and
13. Back-up your data.

You can use the basic version for free or the Premium version for $27.99 annually.

Checklist

If you're after a very simple to-do app with no complicated stuff thrown in, Checklist may be another option for you. The app is all about creating checklists, organizing tasks and sub-tasks, and creating reminders to help you monitor your progress.

Checklist gives you the options of creating unlimited number of checklists and sharing those lists with anybody so you can optimize your personal productivity. Because of its simplicity, you shouldn't have any trouble quickly learning how to use it.

Here are some of checklist's key features, which gives you the ability to:

1. Use built-in templates;
2. Manage tasks and sub-tasks easily;
3. Assign tasks to other people;
4. Create unlimited number of checklists
5. Take notes;
6. Set reminders and due dates for your tasks;
7. Attach files to your tasks;
8. Export your checklists;
9. Set your tasks as one-time or recurring; and
10. Use smart lists to stay on top of your most important tasks.

You can use the free version of Checklist, the Standard version for €3 ($3.94) monthly, the Pro version for €5 ($6.57) monthly, and the Enterprise version for €9.50 ($12.48) monthly.

The Value of Knowing Your Priorities

Before we end this chapter on how to properly use a to-do list to manage your life well, I want to emphasize the importance of knowing your core values or priorities in life. Why? One benefit of doing so is easier and better decision making, especially when it comes to tasks you will take on and prioritize on your to-do list. This can become especially helpful when you're faced with so many things that people expect you to do.

When you know what the truly important things in your life are, such as your life purpose, and the people and things that bring you the most joy, satisfaction and contentment, you won't have to think too much when it comes to deciding which things to say "yes" and "no" to. For example, between a Friday night out with the guys and watching over your 5-year old who is confined in the hospital, it's a no brainer which of the two you'll say "yes" and "no" to, right? That one's easy because the difference in importance is as clear as night and day. But what about when such differences are not that easily distinguished between?

For example, you've been itching to get promoted for more than 5 years now and for the first time in a long while, you feel the favor of the boss is turning in your direction. So, when he tells you to have a round or two at the local bar after hours on Friday, you might be very tempted to tell your wife to move your date because if you turn down your boss, you might let the opportunity to get promoted pass…forever! But then, you're also tempted to say "no" to your boss because it's you and your wife's anniversary on Friday! If your priority is your spouse, which should be the case, it's easy to make the decision to pass up your boss's offer. While it may be hard to tell him about your decision, making the decision itself won't be hard because your priorities are clear in your head. But if you're not sure what your priorities are, you will never be at peace with either decision.

So, take the time to really find out what's most important to you, if you haven't yet. It will make prioritizing tasks so much easier to do.

Chapter 4 - Start By Capturing

As mentioned earlier, one of the biggest benefits of using a to-do list in terms of managing your overall quality of life is the ability to transfer all that information from your head – particularly about the tasks you'll need to finish – onto paper or place it in a digital file. Why is this a benefit again?

You see, keeping so much information that you'll need to remember inside your mind is one of the most stressful things you can do in your life. And considering the fact that our ability to remember and manage information is very limited, no wonder having too many things to try and remember at the right time can be both overwhelming and stressful. With a to-do list, you get to unload stuff from your mind – freeing it up for what really matters! After you've transferred the things you need to do onto a list, you can rest assured that you no longer need to remember them because all you'll need to remember is to look at your list!

I wish I could write a 10,000-word chapter on how to capture the things you'll need to include in your to-do list but, honestly, it's so simple anyone can do it. All you'll really need for capturing the things you need to capture on your to-do list is a clear sense of what's really important to you and the discipline to immediately write down the things you'll need to do on your list the moment you realize that such things should be in your to-do list. It's that simple. Again, knowing your priorities in life will allow you to filter which things need to be entered onto your list and which are unimportant. This will keep you from overpopulating your to-do list with too many, unnecessary things to do that will make you feel overwhelmed later on. Immediately writing down the things that you consider to be worthy of inclusion in your to-do list prevents you from forgetting to do so later on and allows you to immediately let it go from your mind.

Another thing that will help you to consistently capture things in your to-do list is choosing a great app on which you can immediately capture things for inclusion in your to-do list. Personally, I love Wunderlist. Aside from its flexible functionality (you can use it on your smartphone or computer in a synced manner, allowing you enter new items anytime and anywhere), it can also sync to your Google Calendar and iCal accounts!

Again, there's really no secret formula for consistently capturing things to put on your to-do list. It just needs plain and simple discipline and consistency. Just write them as soon as you think of them. It may sound so simple, but it's your only guaranteed way to capture all you need to capture on your to-do list and ensure effective time chunking later on.

Things to Capture

Before thinking about how to capture the things you'll need for populating your to-do lists wisely, you'll need to know what to capture first. Here are some of the most important things you'll need to capture for your to-do lists for optimal time-chunking:

1. Tasks that you can't afford to forget;
2. Tasks that you have to get done within the day;
3. New habits you need to develop like regular exercise;
4. Steps you need to take to accomplish your relatively bigger goals;
5. Menial tasks;
6. Promises you made to other people;
7. Tasks you delegated to others;
8. Tasks you need to do yourself;
9. Tasks with set deadlines; and

10. Answers you're waiting on others for, i.e., follow-ups.

Using Goal-Setting to capture what is Most Important

Right now, you might not be sure which goals are most important to you. Even if you do have a general idea of where your life is going, you may not know how to get there. There is nothing wrong with having the hope that your life will improve one day. It is okay to hope that you will meet the love of your life, start a family, travel, or land your dream job. With only hope and no plan, however, those vague goals you set for yourself are just dreams. And while dreams are not always bad, failing to set goals for your dreams or to take steps toward achieving them makes them nothing but fantasies.

As you consider which activities you want to capture each day, think about what you can do for yourself. What goals do you have and what steps could you take today to reach them? Most days, you'll find there is a tiny step you can take toward your goal. Someone who wants to lose weight is moving closer to their goal every day that they go to the gym and stick to their diet. Someone who wants to earn a promotion works toward their goal by helping solve problems at work and sharing innovative ideas with their boss. A person who is interested in learning how to cook might make an effort to make dinner each night, as practice is the only way to put cooking skills to practice. Even something like looking around online for night classes or trying to find a college online can help you put your goals in perspective and reach for your dream job.

You see, the people who are most successful in achieving their goals are those who are constantly reaching for them. It takes a lot of effort to earn the things that you want in life, especially when there are obstacles in the way. Rather than seeing things as obstacles, look at them as challenges. Consider how you can change your life each day, which challenges you can overcome, and how you can begin building a better future for yourself. You'll find that once you begin making a constant and consistent effort toward the things that you want in life, there is little that can hold you back or stand in your way.

How to Set Goals

Imagine that you are standing in front of a large target that is about fifty feet away. Instead of picking up an arrow, putting it in the bow, and firing ahead, you pick up the arrow and just lob it toward the target. Of course, it misses the target completely, doing a flip in the air and then falling to the ground.

Wanting to achieve something is not enough. When you set goals that are unreasonable or unspecific, you are left holding an arrow without a bow and lobbing it through the air. There is no plan or path, so the arrow cannot follow the forward trajectory to hit that bull's eye. You will never achieve what you want—you might not even know what you want is.

To set goals that will matter as you chunk your time, consider the acronym SMART:

- Specific
- Measurable
- Attainable
- Relevant
- Time-Bound

A specific goal is created through the clarity of your vision. It is not enough to say, "I want to be a better artist." Instead, it would be better to create the goal of getting into an art gallery or selling your first sculpture. If your vision is not clear, then it is impossible to know when you have achieved your goal. You can assume you have improved if you continue practicing art, however, your success would be relative to how you felt about your art piece.

The measurability of your goal helps track progress. For example, weight is something that is easy to measure and track, so a person knows if they are doing well on their diet or if their cheat days have caused them to gain a few pounds. Measurability can also be created using milestones. For example, someone trying to move up the ranks at work might consider a promotion to assistant manager a milestone in their quest to rise to the top in their company.

Something that is attainable describes a goal that is plausible. Poorly chosen goals can have a negative impact on your self-confidence. It is unreasonable for someone who is dieting to expect themselves to lose 50 pounds in a single month—that would be over a pound a day (and incredibly unhealthy). If they expect themselves to reach this goal, they might become discouraged when they only lose 15-20 pounds at the end of the month. This can shake their confidence and make it less likely that they want to continue pursuing their goal. Instead of being unreasonable, set yourself up for success. Remember that many of the goals you set are going to take time to achieve.

Relevant goals describe those that are important to you. Consider the lack of motivation that a college student would have if they were pursuing the law degree that their parents want them to get. Since the student is not doing it for themselves, they will likely struggle through classes and have a hard time motivating themselves to sit through schoolwork. This is not necessarily the student's fault—the goals they have set are misaligned with the things that they truly want out of life. For you to be motivated to reach your goals, therefore, they must be relevant. Otherwise, you may find yourself lacking the motivation to get things done. The letter 'R' is also sometimes referred to as 'rewarding', since the goals you set should be personally rewarding to your life.

Time-bound goals are those that have a deadline. While you should be reasonable with how quickly you expect to reach your goals, setting a deadline keeps you on track. Once you have a main deadline, you can break your goal up into manageable parts and set individual deadlines for those as well. Over time, you'll find that those goals are significantly easier to manage. Something to keep in mind as you work toward goals, however, is that there may be setbacks. Be ready to re-evaluate, come up with a new plan, and change your deadline if it is necessary.

Additional Goal-Setting Tips

Goal-setting should not be something dreadful or unpleasant—it should be motivating. When you are setting goals, you are preparing for the next step in your life. Follow these tips to help you reach your goals:

- Adjust the size of your goals as needed. If you set a goal that is too hard, try to overcome it and adjust for next time. Likewise, if a goal seems too easy, challenge yourself a little more next time. Goal-setting is about balance—you should feel uncomfortable as you do new things and achieve more, but you should not feel discouraged or overwhelmed.
- Change your goals as needed. In addition to the timeline of goals changing, you may find that your priorities change over time. For example, someone who is returning to school might change their plans if

they learn they have a baby on the way. Each time that you want to change your goals, set aside time for personal reflection and meditation. Be sure that you know what next path you want to choose in your life before starting a goal.

- Build new skills as they are needed. Some goals will challenge your skill level, while others will require you to learn new skills. Unfortunately, if you need new skills, you might find you need to set a secondary goal before getting back on the path to your achievement. On the bright side, when you do get to the next part of the goal, the new skill you have learned will still be fresh in your mind.

- Always write your goals down. Even if you don't plan on achieving a goal for five, ten, or even twenty years, it is important to make a record of those things you want to achieve. Without writing the goal down, it is less concrete. It is also more likely that you will push the goal off to the side or forget about the commitment that you have made toward achieving your goals.

- State your goals as a positive statement. Rather than telling yourself what not to do or what you want to avoid, state things that you do want to achieve. For example, don't marry someone who is inconsiderate is a poor choice for a goal. Instead, you would set the goal of marrying someone who is considerate and caring.

- Know where your goals rank in priority. One of the biggest challenges people face as they set several goals for themselves is knowing where to start. Remember that goal setting is not meant to overwhelm you—it is simply meant to help you move in a forward momentum through your life. Think about what matters most to you and what is most achievable now. Then, work toward those goals and set some others aside until later. As you learn to balance the goals you are currently working on and as you overcome milestones, get in the habit of re-evaluating and deciding what steps you want to take next.

How Do I Know Which Goals to Set?

Many people walk through life unsure of what they want to achieve. They may not be sure of their purpose or where they fit into life. The reality is that you can set any goal that you would like to—it does not matter what it pertains to. You are the creator of your own destiny once you take back control of your life, so you can set goals in any area you would like to. Here's a few categories to get you started:

- Attitude- Do you struggle with negative thinking? Is there a part of your mindset that is preventing you from moving toward your goals? Do you have a behavior or habit that upsets you? If so, work to find a solution by setting a goal that will help you manage that problem. You'll find that it is much easier to reach for your goals once you are in the right frame of mind.
- Physical- Do you have any weight gain/loss goals or athletic goals you want to change? Are you trying to change your diet to promote better health or try to sleep better at night? Think about what steps it would take to change your physical health, so you can live to a ripe old age.
- Career- How do you feel at your current job? Do you have a dream job or a specific level that you'd like to reach in your career? Do you want to own your own business one day? Regardless of whether you want to stay in your current organization or find a new job, you can work toward a new career simply by starting your education or learning the skills that you need to excel.
- Skills- Skill goals can involve anything that you want to learn to do better. For example, someone who wants to go into a management job might take

financial classes or work on their people skills. A person who wants to move to a new career field might take steps to further their education. Someone who wants to buy their first car might need to learn to drive first. Skill goals are great starters, as they usually involve something that you can build on to reach later goals.

- Artistic- Are there any specific artistic goals you want to reach? Do you want to learn how to paint or spread your ideas across a different medium? Is there anything special you want to communicate with your art?
- Financial- What type of money do you want to earn in life? What are some of the purchases you plan on making? How much do you need to do those things? What extra money do you plan on making?
- Family/Relationships- Do you see yourself getting married in the future? Do you want to be a parent? What steps would you take to be a good parent? How can you improve the important relationships in your life?
- Education- What skills or information do you need to reach other goals? Is there anything specific that you want to learn?
- Public Service- How do you feel about the world around you? Do you wish you could make it a better place? How would you go about doing that if money was not an option?
- Pleasure- What types of activities do you want to use to enjoy yourself? Is there anything new, fun, and exciting that you want to try for the first time?

If you are having a hard time narrowing down your goals, start by brainstorming 2-3 goals that you could have in each category. These goals should be meaningful and important to you. Once you have brainstormed, start by choosing one of each goal for each category. From here, you can select three, five, or however many goals you are comfortable with. The number of goals you are balancing might also be affected by how challenging each goal is. Do not choose so many that you are overwhelmed. Instead, find a few goals that you are comfortable working with at once. If you do feel overwhelmed, take a look over your list again and decide which goals you want to put off until later. It is better to complete 2-3 goals well than to struggle because you decided to attempt 5 or 6 goals at once.

Finally, remember that the goals you set need to reflect your life. Once you are sure that the goals you are choosing reflect those things you want (not the things your spouse, family, or boss want), break them up into smaller milestones. Set deadlines for each of these milestones and make the goals that you have a reality. Something to keep in mind is that you should have both short-term and long-term goals. It is incredibly useful to reflect on where you want to be ten years from now or five years from now. Of course, it is harder to set a goal for ten years. But when you break that up into years, and then into chunks of several months, and then into a single month, the goals that you want become a reality. Setting goals for the long-term helps you find a bigger picture and reflect on those things that are most important in your life. As you reflect on these things, you'll find that you are consciously making an effort to move toward them. For example, someone who wants to be significantly thinner and healthier in the next year might focus on how their decision will impact them in the future. By thinking about the future and how decisions made now might affect it, this person can set better fitness goals and make better eating choices. Each time that they do this, they bring themselves closer to their goal.

Chapter 5 – Creating Chunks

If you want to successfully manage your life, you will have to successfully manage your time. As I've been repeating, a to-do list is one of the best tools you can include in your time and life-management arsenal. But, of course, having a list of things to do isn't the end goal. After you've captured everything you need to do, what's next? Well, you'll need a strategic way of accomplishing all those tasks.

One thing you'll need to understand when you try to accomplish such tasks is this. Your most important tasks will require significant chunks of uninterrupted time for successful completion. Your ability to successfully accomplish your most meaningful tasks will be greatly dependent on your ability and skills, particularly in creating or blocking out significant chunks of highly productive and valuable time for these tasks. Without these important time chunks, don't expect to be able to successfully accomplish your most important tasks in automatic mode.

If you want to emulate the most successful people on Earth, you'll have to emulate the fact that they always block out considerable chunks of time daily to do the "boring" and "mundane" things that are most important to their success. For sales people, it is cold-calling each and every single day or prospecting. Instead of waiting for prospects to come to them, they go out and look for prospects. For athletes like Stephen Curry, the "boring" stuff involves doing shooting and dribbling drills. You think those from-beyond-the-planet 3-point shots and highlight ankle breakers came by simply visualizing and confessing? No, success came as the result of hundreds of hours of boring and repetitive work at the gym. And guess what? Curry had to – and continues to – set aside significant chunks of time daily to do the mundane and the boring but very important stuff. Some of the greatest businesses minds in history have been known to devote significant amounts of time every day or every week to reading books and learning something new. And some set aside time every morning for meditation and physical exercise for mental and physical energy.

Scheduled Time Blocks; Your Keys to Successful Life and Time Management

If you want to be consistently productive and succeed in everything that you do, you must learn to block off a fixed chunk of time to do specific and very important tasks that will contribute most to your personal and professional success. You must honor your appointments with your own self and be disciplined enough to consistently honor those appointments and block off 30, 60, or more minute segments to work on your most important tasks without interruptions.

One of the things that very productive people do is to divide their working days into pre-planned slots within the day, in which they work on their most important tasks for the day – one at a time – without interruption. By doing so, they avoid multi-tasking and are able to focus on one task at a time, which allows them to work better and faster. By chunking their work into uninterrupted time slots that focus only on one task at a time, they become 3 to 5 times more productive than most average people.

One of the most important tools for optimal productivity is a time planner, which is a planner that's broken down by day and by every half-hour and organized ahead of time. By having a visual break down of each day, you can easily see during which parts of the day you can block off uninterrupted time for deep focus and very important work.

When you're working during these uninterrupted time blocks, it's important to create a working environment that's as distraction-free as possible. To the extent that you can lock your door and put a "don't disturb" sign, turn your phone on to silent or airplane mode, and turn off your computer's Wi-fi. If you need Wi-fi for research or for anything else for your work, make sure that your email and social media accounts are logged off. The last thing you'd want to happen is to see a social media or email notification in the middle of important deep focus work that you find very boring.

Finally, I highly recommend listening to instrumental music only when doing deep focus work. Why? If you listen to songs with lyrics, your mind will be very tempted to sing them, which will distract your focus from your work. That being said, avoid listening to instrumentals of actual songs with lyrics because even if there aren't any lyrics being sung, the familiar tune will trigger your mind to fill in the blanks with the appropriate lyrics and you still end up being distracted. There are plenty of other options. Upbeat classical music is beneficial for stimulating the mind without drawing attention to yourself. Binaural beats are another option. These are sounds that sync your brainwaves to a specific frequency. When working, you can choose a frequency that helps you focus.

Time Chunking

Now, this is where the rubber meets the road. This is where you will start to zone in on just one important task at a time. Doing this will mean that you'll have to exercise a great deal of discipline – at least in the beginning – to work according to schedule regardless of your current state of mind. If you're able to consistently do this, then you'll be able to consistently make significant contributions to your life and your work that will eventually add up to your overall success.

So how do you start your time chunking? Start with the very first item on the list regardless of how boring or uninteresting it feels. Remember, that's why you already prioritized the information you already captured earlier on. By doing so, you eliminate the need to use more mental energy than what is needed by the time you're about to start working on your tasks just to sort out which of the tasks should go first. And if left to your own devices, you will probably choose the tasks that are more interesting but may not necessarily be the most important. You already chose your priorities. As Nike would always say, just do it!

Another key to successful time-chunking is to create very specific chunks of time for your tasks. If you don't make it as specific as possible, you will be at high risk of not being able to concentrate long enough on your important tasks to make any significant impact or headway. Why?

Deciding to allot 1 hour to writing the first 1,500 words of your book project isn't specific enough because then there's the next question of "when" will you schedule that 1 hour of writing 1,500 words? Is it today, this morning, this afternoon, the last 1 hour before going to bed? When? Without a committed time, there's no commitment. When there's no commitment, your chances of actually working on a task becomes very, very low.

The key to being able to successfully employ time chunking is to plan your day ahead. Don't decide on the day itself the exact time slots in which you'll work on specific important tasks. Decide and commit the day before. That way, all you'll need to focus on when the workday starts is just doing those things. For easier organization, choose between 30-minute, 60 minute, and 90-minute time chunks for working on specific tasks.

Time Chunking by Batching

The term "batching" refers to a time management and personal productivity strategy of working on batches of the same or similar tasks in one sitting. For example, freelance writers do several things when it comes to churning out written content for their clients:

1. Outlining content;
2. Writing the content based on the outline;
3. Reviewing the first draft; and
4. Revising the draft, if needed.

If a freelance writer has to churn out 10 articles for the week here's how batching may work for him or her:

1. Monday Morning: create the outlines for all 10 articles;
2. Monday Afternoon to Wednesday Noon: write the first drafts of the articles.
3. Wednesday Afternoon: read through each of the articles and self-edit.
4. Thursday to Friday: Make the necessary revisions before submitting to the client.

The beauty of batching is that it allows you to minimize task switching and distractions while building and maintaining momentum, which can help you get more things done with better quality. You can think of batching as akin to a factory assembly line. Each time that you chunk out a section of time, you should be thinking about the batch of related tasks that can be processed during that time. This means less downtime in between tasks and more productivity on your end. You'll find that each of the things that you have to do in life happens more quickly and that you finally have time to accomplish all the goals that you have set for yourself.

Mega-Batching

This is a mega-sized variation of batching that I learned from the one of the most recognized Internet marketing resource people in the world, Amy Porterfield. Mega-batching involves setting aside huge chunks of time once or twice a week to "batch" process similar huge tasks that tend to be very important but, well, boring.

In Amy Porterfield's example, podcasting is a huge chunk of her business, but it has come to the point when it's become boring and repetitive for her and her team. What she did was to mega-batch the podcast production processes, so it would be more efficient and less cumbersome on her and her team.

For example, part of her podcast production process is the actual recording session. Instead of having to record one episode once every week, she mega-batched it by recording 3 to 4 podcast episodes in one day, once a month only. Since she was already in the recording booth to record an episode, recording 3 more during the whole day means she and her team only has to set up once for the whole month instead of 4 times. That already saved her team a lot of time and got more episodes done for less time.

If you're a blogger, you can also assign one day in a month or every two weeks to write content that's good for a couple of weeks. When you do that, you get to sit down to write less frequently and get more time for other things that matter. Or if you're a health buff, you can prepare your meals for one week in just one afternoon, segregate them in meal-sized containers, and just nuke them in the microwave when you're good to eat or when you need to take them when you go out of the house. Contrast this to preparing your meals every day, which won't be as efficient a use of your time. Instead of chopping and cleaning vegetables several days out of the week, you will only do it once. You also only have to clean up after your cooking once—the rest of the week is just maintenance.

When you get in the habit of setting aside time to meet your goals, it becomes more likely you will be able to achieve them. Think about the valuable time that you waste each time you get distracted. Remember that your mind runs on processing power like a computer, only being able to focus on one task at once. Every time that you let your email pull you away from your stack of paper work or respond to a text message, you are taking away from valuable time that you could be using to improve the quality of your life.

So, get in the habit of doing one thing at a time. Set aside chunks of your day for certain tasks and then commit your time only to those activities. Of course, there will be things that are unavoidable. You might have a client call while you are in the middle of a project or your boss may call you to their office. Your significant other might call you during your workout time and tell you that they need you to pick up the kids after school or take your pet to the veterinarian. You cannot always plan for these unexpected moments that take away from your ability to give what you are doing your full focus. However, you can plan to return your focus as soon as you get a chance.

When you do switch tasks, give your mind time to adjust—it is going to need it anyway. Rather than switching back and forth, take care of those unexpected things that have come up. Then, sit at your work area for several moments with your eyes closed and take deep breaths. You could meditate for a few minutes if you would like to clear and focus your mind. By doing this, you are giving your mind the time it needs to switch between tasks. The amount of time you spend deep breathing is not a loss. You'll find that you work much more productively when your brain has a chance to catch up to what is going on before you get started.

Something else that can help is assigning a specific location to different tasks that you want to complete. For example, assign a specific desk or table in your home to be used any time that you have to bring work home. Try to sit in the same space in your office each time that carry out administrative tasks. Instead of trying to relax by eating in your office (your workspace) on your lunch break, take the time to go for a walk around the building while you eat your sandwich or socially interact with a coworker.

Changing your physical location can drastically help your mind realize that something new is going on. Once you are refocused, you'll find yourself processing information and finishing your tasks faster than you ever have before.

Other Chunking to Benefit Your Life

Have you ever been incredibly motivated to finish something, but gotten hung up on the details? Maybe you had to waste time digging through your notes to find a certain statistic or you were trying to use information you know to come up with a business plan. When you cannot access the information that you have stored in your brain, you cannot possibly expect to use it in a way that can benefit you in the future.

How Memory Works

There are two parts of your memory; short-term or working memory and long-term memory. You can think of your working memory as a type of scratch pad that your mind uses in the moment. It generally consists of information that is important now or in the near future. However, once this information is no longer relevant, the mind will push it to the side.

Something that greatly affects the short-term memory and how likely you are to remember something is the number of things you are trying to store in your short-term memory. The average person cannot remember more than seven things in their short-term memory at once, without their working mind ripping out a page from the sketchpad and tossing it to the side. This is okay, since working memory typically only holds that information while you are still focused on it. Some people only remember things for 10-15 seconds, while others might remember things in their short-term memory for up to a minute.

Once the time is up for the information you have place in your short-time memory, your mind has to make a critical decision about it—should it hold onto that pieces of information and commit it to memory forever? Or should it toss that information to the side? You do have the power to consciously commit information to long-term memory. Otherwise, students would not be able to effectively study for tests. Motivation plays a major role here, as you are going to have trouble committing information to memory if you do not have positive feelings about it. Think about the student who constantly struggles to remember facts about history. They do not have any emotional attachment to this information, so if they are not interested in it, it is going to be that much harder to remember.

Information for short-term memory is stored briefly in the prefrontal cortex of the brain. Interestingly, this is also the area of the mind where information is recalled. Any time that you are working to remember something, you are making that request in your prefrontal cortex. It comes out of the deep recesses of your mind and stays in the prefrontal cortex while you are using it. You can also manipulate information in this area of the brain, either changing it or making connections with other information you have. Then, the information disappears until you need to recall it again later.

Using Chunking for Your Memory

While you can chunk time, you can also get in the habit of chunking pieces of information in your brain. When you chunk information, you can access it much quicker. The human mind can process 'chunks' of information, just like a computer does. This type of chunking only refers to grouping or organizing pieces of information, usually related information that is easy to piece together. There are several strategies you can use to do this, including:

- Grouping- Grouping involves breaking up numbers into more manageable chunks. For example, it would be difficult to chunk ten unrelated numbers together. If you break these ten numbers into five groups of two, however, you greatly increase the chance that you will remember them.
- Patterns- Finding patterns in information gives you the chance to remember the pattern, rather than the individual steps. For example, students may learn PEMDAS as Please Excuse My Dear Aunt Sally. Even though this is a fun way to remember this information, it is actually an acronym that is used to help students remember the order of operations when they are completing math problems (Parentheses, Exponents, Multiplication, Division, Addition, and Subtraction. When you notice patterns, you can come up with acronyms or fun sayings that can help you draw back the memories when you need them.
- Organizing- Organizing information involves chunking based on its meaning or significance. For example, imagine that you were trying to remember the age of twenty people in a group, all ranging from

20 to 25. Instead of trying to recall each person's individual age, you would group them according to their ages first. Then, you would commit each age (the number) and the names of the people who are that age to a group. By doing this, you'll be more likely to remember that Bob is the same age as Suzy, who is 24, so Bob must also be 24.

- Graphic Organizers- Visually organizing information is incredibly helpful for people trying to remember something for later. Consider the saying, "A picture is worth a thousand words." Put simply, this means that in a single photo, you are collecting a great amount of information. You can apply this same principle when trying to remember information or learn something new. Graphic organizers not only chunk ideas together, but they also help you create a connection between the ideas. For example, you might use the a flow chart to remember the business systems life cycle, while it would be better to organize a group of sports in a different manner. When you create these organizers, keep them handy and save them for later. You can take snapshots of these so you can visually recall them. Once you master visual recall, it will be effortless to bring back the information whenever you need it.

- Rehearsal- This is a common studying technique that is used to commit information to memory. Actors and actresses use it when memorizing lines and students use it to study for tests. When you repeat information in your mind many times, it can lengthen the amount of time that it can stay in short-term memory. For example, you might see a phone number on a billboard a few blocks from your house. Instead of writing it down, you repeat it on a loop until you get home. While rehearsal can be beneficial for lengthening the amount of time that you can commit something to working memory, it is not usually the best tactic when you are trying to commit something to long-term memory. Repetition does little to create imagery or invoke emotion in the mind. It also does not group information without conscious effort. Before you can commit something to the long-term, you must be invested. This is the reason that actors use emotions and movements while they are rehearsing lines. By physically acting out the scene and becoming emotionally invested in it, they are more likely to perform their lines.

- Creating Connections- The brain is an incredible network of tissues and neurons, which somehow comes together to help us form thought processes. Each time that you have a unique thought, your mind follows a specific path of neurons to get there. This means that when you can effortlessly remember something, you can make it easier to remember other information by tying it into what you already know. As you learn new materials and reach for your goals, try to create connections to those things you already know. Instead of struggling to commit them to memory, your mind will associate them with something that already has a deep significance in your mind.

Creating a Memory Palace

Another technique commonly used by some of the most intelligent people in the world is creating a memory palace. You can think of a memory palace as a sort of library where you can access any of the information you have consciously committed to your brain. A memory palace does not necessarily have to be an actual palace—it is actually best if you use a location that you can easily remember the details of. Even though this can be a fictional place or somewhere you have never visited, rehearsing this location is important. If you cannot remember the small details about it, it makes it nearly impossible to form the connections that you need to for creating solid memories.

If you are familiar with the BBC show Sherlock Holmes, then you might already have an understanding of what a memory palace is. He often goes deep into his memory palace and finds critical connections between information (which he then usually uses to solve crimes or save the day). While this might be considered something of fantasy for people who have never attempted this practice, creating a memory palace is actually quite achievable. Everyone has the ability to create a memory palace—few people have knowledge of the techniques needed to achieve this.

Before you begin storing information in your memory palace, you should draw a physical map of where you plan to store this information. The key is to select a location that you know well and that has many details. For example, you might remember information by planting it in little garden plots in the park that you visit or choose to store information in one of your favorite fantasy worlds. It does not matter what the location is, as long as you can see it vividly in your mind and you will be able to recall it.

Drawing the mind map is important because it gives you a sense of direction. It does not necessarily have to be pretty—it just needs to point you the way you need to go. Next, take the time to write down a detailed walkthrough. Start at the entrance of your location or map and write down the small details. If you were using your childhood home, for example, you might walk through the door and notice the umbrella stand in the corner, a pile of shoes, and a clock. While you did create the outline of this space with your initial drawing, now is the point where it is important to take the details down. Each of these details will have relevance as you continue to move on.

Once you have entered the front hallway of your childhood home and taken stock of the things there, move down the hallway to the kitchen or walk up the stairs and explore. You are going to go room-by-room in your memory palace, writing down details of each area. While this might seem tedious or excessive, think of this as a wise investment of your time. By being detailed now, you are making it more likely that you will experience success in the future. Think about the external part of the mind palace as the skeleton. Simply visualizing the place isn't enough to make it work—a skeleton does nothing but lie there. By adding details to your memory palace, you are providing it with the skin and internal organs that it needs to function.

Once you have a detailed outline of your memory palace and those things that are inside of it, you can start building a collection of things that you would like to remember. Use the individual rooms in your memory palace to separate information according to topic or relevance. For example, you might walk outside of your childhood home and notice the garden. In this garden, you could 'plant' your collection of information about edible plants in case you are ever in a survival situation or for times when you go camping. Here, you might visualize both the plant and a name tag for it, so you know its name and what it looks like.

Like the garden, you can use this technique to remember anything. If you are trying to remember the ingredients to your grandmother's family cookie recipe, you might walk into the kitchen, open the oven, and pull out a cookie sheet that you have 'placed' there with all the ingredients you need laid out on it, measured out in spoons and measuring cups. This helps you visualize this information as if you are actually living it and helps it come more vividly in your mind. Instead of pondering constantly over what ingredient you are missing, you can pull the baking sheet from the oven and feel confident that you have not left anything out of your grandmother's cookie recipe.

The bottom line is that chunking anything in your life is going to save you time. Think about how much smoother your computer runs once it has been defragmented and optimized. For people who want to achieve the most in their lives, it is important that you do not waste time switching between tasks. This time could be better spent elsewhere—even if you are only using that extra 25 minutes you have each day to meditate, read a good book, or take a long walk. It does not matter what you are doing this at this time—it is just a luxury to have it to do something that you enjoy rather than wasting it on meaningless tasks.

Chapter 6 – Allocating Your Time Better

Everyone has the same 24 hours in a day. Then, why is it that the other stay-at-home mom in your life has time to go to the gym and go out with the ladies once per week, while you barely keep up with the housework? Why is it that the guy in your office with the sloppiest handwriting brings in the most revenue? The reality is that these people do not have more time than you—they have just chosen to use their time differently. They have decided to put their all into the things that really matter to them, rather than worrying about excelling in every area of their life.

Put simply, the people who excel at getting the things they need to do done during the day are not perfectionists. They know where their effort is going to be most appreciated and most rewarded. Stop thinking of time as something that you can get 'more' of anytime you run out of it. That time has to come from somewhere. Staying up late to finish a project means less sleep and less productivity the following day. Even though the project is done, you have still negatively impacted the amount of time that you have left. By using the following strategies, you can allocate your time better and more effectively, so you can get the most out of your life.

Know Your Strengths

Take a moment and think about something that you frequently do but are not really good at. For example, you might struggle with creating emails, so you frequently spend a lot of time looking over them because you are not confident in your abilities. Or, perhaps you are horrible at keeping records but you do the time-consuming work yourself instead of sending it over to the accounting department, believing that it will make you stand out to your boss. When you do something that you know you are not good at, your confidence is already slightly shaken. You may work on it slower than other tasks because you want to be sure it is perfect—but this takes away valuable time that you could be doing an activity you are great at—and doing it effectively.

Of course, there are always unpleasant tasks that you must do yourself. However, when you shine in another area, let that stand out. Do not obsess over those things that you may not do well. Instead of worrying about finding the perfect wording for a business email, give it a quick proofread for errors and hit the send button. Email is a two-way street. If the other person needs further clarification or they have questions about the way you wrote the email, they will contact you with a follow-up. When you do not have to do those activities (like inputting expenditures that are normally handled by the accounting department), let someone else do them.

Not only does knowing your strengths help you cut back on the amount of time you spend doing unpleasant tasks, but it also helps you shine in those areas where you excel. There is a reason that your boss doesn't give your coworker crap for the occasional typo in emails—they might excel at coming up with unique solutions or entertaining clients. The reason people have unique job titles is because they have unique skills. When you stop doing those things you don't have to do, especially when you are not good at them, you are leaving yourself plenty of time to stand out in a way that isn't so difficult.

Learn to Set Boundaries

It can be difficult to say 'no' when your date asks you to stay for 'just one more drink' or your boss asks you to stay 'just one more hour.' When you are chunking your time, however, that extra hour spent either playing or working takes away an hour somewhere else. Every moment of your time is valuable. Other people often do not realize that. Your date thinks it is okay because you are having a good time while your boss thinks it is okay because you get paid for that extra time.

However, people are rarely as respectful of your time as you are. Even people like your significant other or your parents, who often mean well, can take away from that precious time you have already allocated to different areas of your life. Unless you set clear boundaries, you cannot expect anyone to respect your time. They might see it as just a little more of your time, without realizing that they are taking away from something you have already committed yourself to.

The best way to set boundaries is to know what you need and what you have planned—then communicate that message to the people around you. If you do commit to something like helping a friend move on the weekend, be sure to set out your schedule ahead of time. If you can only help them move for two hours, let them know that you have another commitment. If your parents want you to visit but you only have a spare hour, let them know that before your visit.

Keep in mind that there will always be someone who has a hard time accepting the boundaries you are setting. Your parents may protest when you have to leave after an hour-long visit and your boss may beg you to put in the extra time. Remember that even when there are important people in your life, the time that you have is ultimately your own. If you allow other people to continue to push your own life aside and do things their way, they are going to continue to pester you each time they want something more. If you give them a firm 'no' and stick to it, they will eventually learn that you value your own time. While they are a valuable asset in your life, there are other obligations that you must attend to if you want to be the best and happiest version of yourself.

Remember you are a priority in your life. While it is easy for other people to believe that you 'owe' them your time, you must make time for yourself or you are going to be miserable. When you live your life in accordance with what other people want, instead of realizing the things that you want, it can cause a great deal of misery. You may find that your life lacks meaning or that it is harder to find the motivation you need to get things done. Furthermore, by avoiding the things you need to do for yourself, you are sending the message that you do not care about those things you want to achieve. You are setting yourself aside for other people. While some people call this selfless, there is a line that must be drawn. Otherwise, people will take advantage of your selfless nature and try to control your life. Rather than being happier or having a greater payoff, you will be left feeling exploited and as if your efforts have been in vain, because they have not contributed to your life in any way.

As you consider where to spend your time, you must also consider which relationships you want to invest your time in. Not every relationship that you have in your life is going to be mutually beneficial. There are always people at work or at home that will prey on people who are naturally kind and giving to convince them to contribute to their lives. You can help these people out sometimes, especially when they need it most. However, if it comes out that you are always helping and the other person does not attempt to benefit your life in any way, then you might want to re-evaluate who you are spending time with. Instead, let these negative relationships go in favor of those that are more fulfilling in nature. Surround yourself with people who are motivated and determined to get their own work done, even when they are struggling. Surround yourself people who will lend a helping hand when you need one, even if it is just listening to you vent about work or going for a walk with you to distract you from the long day you have had.

Develop Confidence Where You Need it

It does not do any good to beat yourself up over skills that you do not have. Imagine how upsetting it would be to be passed over for a promotion because your competitor has graphic design abilities that let them put together nicer presentations. When you are passed over and learn why, you have a few options. Most people will be upset momentarily. However, they might understand the reasoning behind their boss' selection. Rather than letting this upset take over, use this as motivation to learn a new skill in life. If being able to create graphic organizers and photos will help you rise to the top in your place of work, then why not do it?

You cannot always avoid doing the things that you do not feel confident in. If you want your boss to recognize you for your great ideas, for example, it doesn't make much sense to avoid giving presentations or sharing information in meetings. Instead, develop that skill enough so that you are confident enough to use it. Once you have done this, you'll find that you can do just about anything you set your mind to.

Decide Where You Don't Want to Spend Time

Things like old commitments that we do not have time for any longer or things we feel obligated to do often get in the way of those things that let us invest in our own lives. For example, you might feel guilty about hiring someone to do the gutters instead of doing them yourself. After all, the only thing that you need to clean the gutters is your time. Instead of feeling guilty, think about all the other things you could accomplish in those hours you would have spent cleaning the gutters. Don't you think the return of your time is worth the investment of paying someone else to do the job that you don't enjoy anyway? You could spend your Saturday fishing or going to the beach instead.

Something else that you can consider as you decide where to spend your time is apps that automate certain processes. For example, you might download an app that helps balance your checkbook every time you make a purchase instead of sitting down and spending an hour doing it manually at the end of each week. Rather than reading over each email you send out several times, download a spelling/grammar checker that helps you pinpoint errors. While it is not foolproof, odds are you can get away with reading through your email for errors once instead of six different times.

Clearing your schedule of tasks that you are not interested in also involves stopping those things that are no longer priorities. For example, someone who joined a club several years ago might not enjoy being a member as much as they used to. However, they have grown fond of the people there and feel obligated to continue their commitment simply for that reason. If they are no longer interested in the activity, whether it is hunting, reading, archery, knitting, gardening, or something else, then it no longer serves a purpose for them. When something seems more of a hassle than an enjoyment, it is time to let it go, regardless of how long you have been doing it.

Make Time Investment a Habit

Automatic time investment is those activities that you set goals for yourself for each week. They should reflect your priorities and those things you feel obligated to accomplish. For example, you might make it a habit to invest an hour to the gym at least three times per week. Someone who enjoys making art for stress relief might invest two hours each week in being creative. A mother or father might commit to spending at least two hours with each of their kids on the weekends.

The purpose of automatic time investment is to keep you aligned with your goals each week. It is important to do things like spend time with your family, keep up with your interests, and stay active. By allocating your time to that and doing it religiously, you have the opportunity to create a habit. Habits are beneficial because they tap into the brain and eventually make it significantly easier to commit to your activities. For example, a parent that makes a habit of checking their child's bookbag every day when they come home is less likely to forget than a parent who checks their child's bookbag whenever they get around to it. Likewise, someone who gets up and goes for a run every morning might feel incomplete if they wake up late and have to start the day without it.

When you do something on the same schedule each day, it forms the connection between that time and the activity. The major benefit of this is that when that time comes around, your brain is in the right mindset to do what you have set out to do. This is the reason it is beneficial to exercise or meditate at the same time each day—your brain is motivated to exercise or calm enough to meditate because it knows that is what it is supposed to be doing during that time.

Analyzing and Optimizing Your Work

So, how do you go about deciding which tasks you should put more effort into and which obligations you should give less effort to? Separate the responsibilities you have each day into three categories; investment, neutral, or optimize.

The investment activities are those where you could have a greater payoff if you give the area more of your time and attention. For example, you may want to put more time into coming up with fresh ideas to show yourself as being an asset at the company you work for, possibly earning a raise or promotion in the process. Strategic planning, whether you are deciding how to best spend your money at the grocery store or which goals you want to meet next week, is another investment where putting in the time and effort pays off. Do not think of a payoff as being purely material either—spending a night out with good friends or having quality time with the people you love without electronics both pay off in the relationships that you are nurturing. You could also consider investment activities as A-level activities, as these are the areas where you want to put in the most work. This means that when you are doing these activities, you fully believe they are worth your time and that they will payoff exponentially. Give these areas your full attention and do them to the best of your ability.

Neutral activities describe those that need to get done. They are not necessarily significant or beneficial. However, they are tasks that cannot be avoided. Neutral activities do not offer a bigger payoff, meaning you are not going to increase your return just by putting more time and effort in. Some of these tasks might be obligations. Neutral activities might be going to the gym or attending project meetings. While they cannot be avoided, you should aim for B-level work. This means you give them only the amount of time they need, but nothing more. It is also okay if you do not perform perfectly in these areas, as they are not going to have the same significant value as A-level work will have in your life.

Optimize activities describe those that you should get done as quickly as possible. Typically, these are considered C-level tasks where you should only put in the minimal effort to get done. These activities are often necessary, mundane tasks that take away from the things that may benefit your life. For example, doing administrative paperwork or running errands for the office should be done as quickly as possible so you can get back to the tasks that really matter.

As you organize your tasks in this way, keep in mind that your overall goal is to give yourself time in your life where you need it most. You should not feel like you are losing anything—those tasks you are only putting partial effort into do not add value to your life and your time does not result in a payoff. Instead, try to choose investment activities to spend the majority of your time on. These are the types of activities that will lead to a happier, more successful life.

Organizing Your Week According to Priority

At the beginning of each week, write down all the investment activities that you want to get to. This includes time you want to spend with your family, time you want to spend on yourself, and work activities that deserve your attention. Make a note of these activities and budget your time so you do these early in the week and early in the day. When you get the important things done earlier, you guarantee that you are investing your time wisely each day. Even though you will like still have neutral and optimize tasks left, you can do them in the time remaining and still feel satisfied that you have accomplished your major goals in the day.

Next, when you create a to-do list each day, label each activity with an "I", "N", or "O". Consider how much time it will take to do each task and budget the day. For example, you might budget the day so you spend eight hours on investment activities (five hours of working on an important project, one hour of time for yourself, and two hours of time for your family), five hours on neutral activities (one hour on going to the gym, one hour on showering after work, one hour on cleaning the house, and two hours in a business meeting), and two hours on optimize activities (thirty minutes answering emails and ninety minutes doing paperwork). By organizing the activities, you can easily adjust if you find yourself going over the allotted time. This is another major benefit of getting investment activities done first. It is much easier to take time for the neutral or optimize categories and give it to important tasks, rather than taking away from your investment activities to give your time to tasks that do not really pay off in the long run.

Chapter 7 – Chunking Work vs. Play

When you consider how to chunk your time, do you make time for play and relaxation? It is easy to become overwhelmed by everything life demands. Consider a mother who goes to work, then comes home, helps the kids with homework, and makes dinner or a father who goes to work and then spends hours in the garage working on the car. Odds are, both of these parents are exhausted by the time they finally have a free moment in their day. They are not focused on enjoying themselves or relaxing—they just want to go to bed.

Unfortunately, it is possible to work too hard. When you constantly push yourself to work harder without taking time to enjoy the fruits of your labors, it can be mentally draining. It stresses out your body and your mind. It may even make it harder to motivate yourself to keep moving forward and maintain a steady flow of pace when you are doing work.

Time Chunking and Balance

Without balancing work and play, you'll quickly find yourself exhausted and beat down. Many people are stuck on the concept of hard work and how it means that you must put every bit of your energy into achieving greatness. With this mentality, however, it makes it almost impossible to enjoy your life. We always feel like we have to work—even when a business email comes in late in the evening, after we have already settled down to watch our favorite movie or the game we have been looking forward to. Rather than staying focused on relaxation, most people hear that email chime as a call to work—unread work emails can't wait until tomorrow, right?

Wrong. That work email could wait until tomorrow. When you are sitting down for that time you have chunked out to enjoy yourself, ignore that call-to-duty from your persistent email tone. Instead, enjoy your movie or game and remind yourself of all the reasons it is important to relax.

All Work and No Play Leads to Health Problems

People who work long hours often justify it by stating that they are going to work hard to make money now and retire and have enjoyment later. However, it is not enough to plan to enjoy your life someday. You must make time for enjoyment and relaxation now.

A life without any time for pleasure leads to stress. When you are stressed, it can cause overwhelming feelings as you think about all the tasks ahead of you. This leaves your mind in a state of panic—which is far from where you want to be when you are trying to focus on the tasks ahead of you. Not only does it take a toll on your productivity, but living with all work and no play also has negative health repercussions. This is especially true for people who lead high-stress lives, regardless of whether the stress comes from their social life, work, or their home life.

People who live with high levels of stress may not realize what is causing their symptoms. They may assume their insomnia, irritability, and headaches are just typical responses of life. Even though these symptoms are not usually debilitating in any way, they decrease productivity and make it harder to maintain focus. Stress also greatly affects the internal workings of the body. Even when the effects are not immediately apparent, they can take a toll on the course of your life. Some common health problems that are a byproduct of managing too much stress include high blood pressure, heart disease, diabetes, and obesity. These are problems that worsen over time. In people who do not closely monitor their health, these often take hold before they realize it is an issue. Here are some of the ways that stress can harm your body:

- Change in sexual interest levels/libido

- Frequent anger or irritability
- Loss of interest in activities
- Eating more or less, poor eating habits
- Fatigue
- Muscle pain and tension
- Headache
- Chest pain
- Insomnia and other sleep problems
- Anxiety
- Depression/sadness
- Feelings of being overwhelmed
- Decreased focus or motivation
- Abuse of drugs and/or alcohol
- Social withdrawal

These symptoms may come and go, depending on the amount of stress that a person is under and their natural response to that stress. Some people can adapt better to new situations and may be less stressed as a result. However, many of these symptoms become problematic as time goes on. Even though it might not seem like too big of a deal if you lose sleep a few nights a week, this lost sleep can lead to increased irritability and difficulty focusing at work. In turn, you will not get as much done and you will put off relaxation time for after you are caught up. This can become a vicious cycle, especially if you remain insistent on catching up with work before you relax every time.

Additionally, long-term poor sleep habits and unhealthy food choices can lead to problems like diabetes and obesity. Long-term stress also heightens your risk of heart problems, like heart attack and stroke, and increases your risk of high blood pressure. It is a slippery slope, which is the reason it is so pertinent that you set aside time in your schedule for those activities that help you relax and enjoy your life.

How to Chunk Work vs. Play

As you chunk work time and playtime, remember that you must separate the two. It can be easy to have overlap, especially as you find yourself sitting at your desk saying you will leave work after you finish 'one more thing' and put off your relaxation for the evening. Instead, when you set yourself a deadline, respect that the time you set aside for work is over. Give yourself permission to relax and enjoy yourself, even when your work is not quite finished or you are not as far as you would like to be. After you relax, you'll find your mind is well-rested and better prepared for being productive anyway.

Another major thing to remember is that you must leave your work at work. For stay-at-home parents, this means avoiding picking up junk from the living room or folding a load of laundry during those times you have set aside for yourself. If you work from home, find an area to designate as your workspace and do not touch that area until you are ready to work.

While you do not have to play every night of the week, you should at the very least make time to do something pleasurable. This could be reading a chapter from a book you enjoy before bed or spending time with someone you care about. It could even be as simple as indulging on a piece of chocolate cake or treating yourself to a coffee at the end of a long day. You do not always have to carve a significant amount of time out of your day to experience pleasure, so making it a habit can drastically improve the happiness and balance in your life.

Active vs. Inactive Activities

There is nothing wrong with staying home and enjoying the football game you have been looking forward to or binge-watching a couple episodes of your favorite television show. For these types of activities to be considered useful in helping manage stress, however, they have to be used in addition to active enjoyment activities. Active relaxation is doing something that benefits you. Even though it might seem that binging on video games or television shows is a great way to relax since you do not have to put in much physical effort, these types of activity are actually stressful over time. When you are staring at a screen, your mind is still processing the information in front of you. It is also a strain on your eyes, which can quickly become worn out if you work at a job where you are frequently looking at a screen.

There is nothing wrong with inactive activities in moderation. However, when you are trying to de-stress, these inactive relaxation strategies often leave you feeling unfulfilled. Even if you won a game or were entertained by the television show, it can still leave you feeling like you haven't really relaxed at all. Better activities are those that get you moving or encourage you to be social. It is better to be entertained by seeing a movie with a friend than binge-watching television alone. Likewise, it is better to go out and play sport or do yoga than inactively sit and play video games on the couch.

As you are chunking your time, remember that you should make time for those things that help you relax, while still providing benefit. For example, activities like going to the gym, playing a sport with a friend, or doing yoga provide physical benefits. Activities like going to the movies with a friend, having a coffee date, and going to a party all have social benefits. You should also make time for things that relax you naturally, like taking a long, hot bath or shower to relax your muscles or reading a book before bed.

Curbing Stress in a Healthy Way

When people hear the word 'stress,' they often associate it with negative feelings and a sense of being overwhelmed. However, the reality is that everyone experiences stress in their lives. Stress can be positive or negative. For example, when someone who is trying to get pregnant is finally successful, they might be excited about being able to conceive, but stressed about the upcoming expenses and lifestyle changes. Even something like marrying the love of your life that is typically filled with joy is still filled with the stress that comes with change. Marrying the love of your life can change your living situation or how you appear in social circles. While this is not necessarily a bad thing, it is still a change that causes stress.

Curbing stress in a healthy way means giving your body and mind the opportunity to use the stress in a positive way instead of creating panic. For example, imagine that two people are giving a presentation in front of a group of business associates. The presentation could mean standing out as a key role of the team and even a possible promotion. It is obvious that both of the people are stressed, as this is an important presentation and they want to do well.

The first person doesn't use their stress. Instead, they let it control them. When they think of giving their presentation or sharing their ideas, they tense up. They are not focused on the positives that can come out of the meeting, instead being worried that they will stumble over their words or their boss will not like their ideas. They are so stressed about the situation that they start to panic, which makes it hard for them to begin the presentation. On the day leading up to their big moment, they are not spending their time going over their ideas or building their confidence. Instead, they are thinking of all the ways it can go wrong. This person has let their stress control them. When they are standing in front of the audience, the adrenaline and their perception of this moment as something to be feared causes them to panic. They may sweat, stumble over their words, or freeze up completely.

The second person learns to harness their stress in a way that helps them perform better. Stress helps the body respond in tense situations, preparing it to either flight or flight its way through danger.

When you see stress as a natural response to new situations in life, however, you can begin looking at them as opportunities instead of dreading them. When a person who is confident in handling stress has a presentation, they are more likely to perform well. They do not procrastinate when assembling the project and doing research, because they are excited about the potential that the opportunity has. Right before they give their presentation, they are using their stress to help them stay focused and perform well. They are much more likely to have success than the first person who allowed their stress to control their performance. This is not because the second person didn't feel stressed, but because they used that stress to help them focus on their goals and looking at the situation in a positive light instead of allowing that stress to overwhelm them.

How Time Chunking Helps Manage Stress

People who are best adapted to handle stress are those who have made time for work and play in their lives. Have you ever approached someone who seemed really busy and asked them for something? Many times, when someone is hyper-focused on the many tasks in front of them, everything else seems like an annoyance. This means they are more likely to snap and become irritated than help the person who is trying to add to their workload.

When you begin to manage your life by time chunking, especially by balancing work and play, you'll find yourself better prepared to manage stress. You'll learn more about planning your time and managing the things that you must do in life. You also learn to take more time out of your day for yourself, even on those days when you feel like you have so much going on that you couldn't possibly find some time for yourself. Additionally, time chunking manages stress because it gives you the opportunity to lay out your schedule as you see fit. Even though there are tasks that you must do, you have the chance to spread them out in a way that they do not overwhelm you.

Don't Forget to Make Time to Do Nothing

When you are scheduling work and play, don't forget to save yourself time to do nothing. This down time could be a period when you go for a walk on your lunch break or it could just give you ten minutes of sitting somewhere and meditating to relax your mind. The major benefit of making time for nothing is that you free up time for yourself to think about where you are at in life. It can be used as a period of reflection where your mind is finally quiet enough that you can understand your unique wants, needs, and desires. It is during this time when you are most likely to realize the errors of the path you are on so you can readjust or where you can see the next step you need to take in your life.

Living a Mindful Life

Earlier, it was mentioned that being more mindful in life can drastically help you stop 'unplugging' from life. The demands of the average person's life can leave them stressed and overwhelmed. This only gets worse as you obsess over the things that you have to do and worry constantly about not getting them done or not performing well enough. Living a mindful life is as simple as learning to fully immerse yourself in everything you do. Rather than listing off everything that you have to do that day on the way to work, you stop and notice the flowers that are blooming in the park or the happy dog that is running down the sidewalk. Instead of letting your mind wander when you are doing chores or cleaning, you pay attention to the way your muscles move as you sweep the floor. Rather than obsessing over the day you had while in the shower, spend that time to relax and unwind. Pay attention to how the water feels as it runs down your skin and cleanses you of the day and how the hot water penetrates your sore muscles.

By being more mindful, you will find yourself appreciating the things that you do more. Something that once seemed small and mundane like making your bed or taking a shower becomes more significant in your life. You begin to appreciate the work that it takes and that you have done that work.

Mindfulness meditation can also be used as a strategy to invoke relaxation in those times when you need a mental break. It is a refreshing way to reboot your mind when you are under stress. One of the major benefits of mindfulness is that nobody has to know you are doing it. You can be mindful when eating a sandwich or mindful when watching a beetle crawling along your windowsill. What truly matters with being mindful is that you are fully immersed in what you are doing. Rather than thinking about it, you are actually experiencing it. Mindfulness can be thought of as a type of immersion in this way—you want to fully immerse yourself into whatever you are doing at the time.

Try this on your lunch break with a sandwich. When you are making your sandwich at home, take the time to consider the balance of ingredients. Include things with different textures and contrasting flavors, like soft meat and cheese, creamy condiments, juicy tomatoes, and crunchy lettuce. You could also easily do this with a salad. As you eat your lunch, do not obsess over what is in the sandwich or salad. Instead, obsess over the experience. Let the flavor combinations play around on your tongue and experience the textures.

You can apply this same technique to nearly any activity to help you relax. When watching the beetle on the windowsill, for example, you should not be questioning what type of beetle it is or wondering where it is going to travel from here. Instead, notice the shine as the sun hits the beetle. Pay attention to the way that it moves, crawling quickly but making it only a short distance because of its little legs. When it flies away, notice the way that its wings move and how the beetle almost vibrates.

Think of being mindful as a mini-vacation. You can do it with any of your senses—the key is simply getting in the habit of observing without judging. You should be involved with what is going on around you, but not so involved that you worry about it or become stress. Here's a few ideas for what you could do mindfully with each of the senses:

- Touch- Notice the texture of the leather in your office chair, rub your face against one of your favorite blankets, or mindfully pet an animal.
- Sight- Watch how tree leaves blow in the wind or pay attention to the movement of clouds across the sky. It is okay to notice shapes in the cloud—just don't let your mind go off on a distracted tangent. You could also watch the flame of a candle.
- Smell- Breathe in the aroma that comes from the bottom drawer of your wooden desk or the body wash you use. Breathe deeply and truly enjoy the scent as you do.
- Taste- Chew a new piece of gum or a unique-flavored candy. Fully experience your food every time that you eat.
- Sound- Pay attention to the singing of the birds in the morning. Listen to a genre of music you have never heard before and just listen, without judging it. Notice the instruments and the pace of the musician's voice.

Of course, this is not an all-inclusive list. There are many activities in your life that you can do mindfully. As you do this, your mind will be clearer and more relaxed, ready to handle any of the time chunking tasks you are throwing at it.

Other Tips for Finding the Balance between Work and Play

Even when you are time chunking, it can be hard to focus on one thing at a time. Humans are creatures of habit and you'll naturally find yourself trying to answer text message at work or check your email during time you're supposed to be enjoying yourself. These tips can help you as you learn to balance work time and fun time in your life:

1. Combine work and play by organizing a social activity with coworkers. There are plenty of options—a field day with games, a picnic or amusement park outing, a wellness walk, or a service project. This can let everyone get to know each other in a less stressful setting.
2. Find a fulfilling hobby. Taking care of a pet or growing a garden can be a lot of work, but it also has a lot of reward. Some other options include deep breathing activities, painting, writing, or another art outlet, or involving yourself with martial arts or an exercise routine.
3. Plan a vacation a few times a year. Vacationing does not have to be expensive and you do not have to go anywhere. Plan a 'stay'cation and camp in your backyard or spend a couple days lounging with cool drinks at the beach. You could also explore bike paths or nature trails in your area. The key to vacationing is to leave the cell phone behind—pick up a disposable camera for taking pictures instead.
4. Challenge yourself to have fun. Make it a goal to have fun or exercise at least 22 days out of the month. You'll notice a drastic difference in the way that you live your life.
5. Stop making yourself feel guilty for enjoyment. It can be easy to criticize yourself when you are behind schedule with something or your house is messy. However, if you are constantly criticizing yourself for those things that you don't get done, you'll find it is nearly impossible to get the relaxation time that you need for your mind to function at its peak. You should never feel guilty for indulging a little or letting yourself have that enjoyment, especially when you are working your hardest. It is possible that you are behind schedule because you put too much on your plate—it doesn't have to mean anything about your productivity or your work ethic.

Chapter 8—Other Time-Chunking Optimizers

As part of the implementation of time chunking or working on the actual tasks themselves, there are 3 things that can help you optimize your productivity: the 5-Second Rule, the Pomodoro Technique and realizing that multi-tasking is prohibited.

The 5-Second Rule

Popularized by self-help and personal productivity guru Mel Robbins, the 5-Second rule states that if you don't want your primitive brain to kill your instinct to work on a goal or a task, it is best that you physically act on that task within the first 5 seconds of thinking about it. Beyond that, the chances of your brain successfully hijacking you into procrastination become much, much higher. So, the instant you feel a push or a nudge to act on accomplishing a task or a goal, use the rule to launch yourself immediately into action and minimize your procrastination risks.

So how do you implement the 5-Second Rule? As soon as you feel procrastination creeping in and rearing its ugly head when you know you need to act immediately, simply count backward from 5 to 1, much like how NASA and Space-X countdown to their rockets' launches. When you get to 1, just spring into action. It's that simple.

Within that 5 second window lies an eternity of battle between your instinct to act and your mind's tendency to preserve itself via inaction. Outside that 5-second window, your mind has the upper hand. That's why if you don't act within the first 5 seconds upon feeling the temptation to procrastinate, you're toast!

But why the need to count? Well, counting gives your mind something to focus on and will help distract you from the internal struggle to procrastinate with all manner of excuses. While it seems very simple, it's actually one of the most effective ways to push yourself out of your comfort zone and into the discomfort zone of doing hard things that can contribute a lot to your life. You know, the boring, uninteresting, or scary things. Observe this rule and you will experience continuous success in life. Ignore this and you're toast because you will allow procrastination to get a grip on your mind and keep yourself from doing the things you really ought to be doing for a meaningful and successful life.

To get a better appreciation for the 5-Second Rule, let's take a look at its key components. The first component is your instinct moment. And by instinct, I don't mean rash decisions that are often permanent, like the instinct to tell everybody in your favorite watering hole that "the next 10 rounds are on me!" after you've already downed 10 bottles of beer in the last 30 minutes. Instincts are – as Mel Robbins defines them – any impulses, urges, temptations or knowledge that you should either do or not do something about based on gut feelings.

For the purposes of optimal personal productivity, we speak of instincts to act on specific tasks or goals that are important and – well – productive. These include waking up early in the morning to get in your morning run or picking up the phone to do cold-call prospecting if you're a salesman or woman.

The second component of the 5-Second Rule is acting on a goal. This component is crucial because it qualifies which types of instinct you should use the rule on. In particular, you should use the 5-Second Rule on goals or task-related instincts. The earlier example of waking up early in the morning to get your morning run in for improved health and energy is a goal-oriented instinct upon which it'll be good to apply the 5-Second Rule. The instinct to smoke a cigarette is an example of an instinct that shouldn't be acted upon because not only is it unrelated to any worthy goal or task, it's also bad for your health.

The third component of the 5-Second Rule is pushing yourself to action. The reason that the 5-Second Rule exists is because the tendency to procrastinate and not act can be very strong for anybody. If you don't push yourself, you will succumb to the insidious temptation to frequently procrastinate on your most important goals or tasks. When you make procrastination a habit, don't expect to get anything meaningful done on a regular basis and as a result, don't expect any success in life.

The 5-Second Rule – in essence – is about pushing yourself especially during times when you don't want to act outside of your comfort zone. It's about taking hold of the steering wheel of your life and steering it in the direction it needs to go, one push at a time.

Make no mistake about it, the 5-Second Rule is anything but easy. Again, the reason for the 5-Second Rule is to push you out of complacency and procrastination, both of which are easy but deadly for your personal and professional successes. When the moment comes when you suddenly feel the instinct to act in ways that will contribute to your success and allow you to accomplish your goals or tasks, your primitive brain will awaken from its stupor and will do whatever it can to convince you to kill those instincts. All it needs to successfully murder those instincts is a little over 5 seconds. That's why within the first 5 seconds upon feeling the instinct to act on your goals or tasks, you should launch yourself into physical action. Beyond 5 seconds, it's a losing battle.

The fourth component is action within the time frame, which is the first 5 seconds. But there's something you'll need to understand about "action" or "acting" within the first 5 seconds. These don't mean you'll have to do something grandiose to immediately accomplish your goals or tasks. What action means in this context is to start physically moving in the direction of your instincts, goals or tasks.

Let's use the example of getting your morning run in again. When your alarm goes off, you have 5 seconds within which to set yourself in the direction of your goal or task, which is to get ready for a run. Within 5 seconds, you can do that by simply turning off your alarm and getting up to wash your face in the bathroom within the first 5 seconds upon waking up from the alarm. You don't have to hit the road within the first 5 seconds, but by turning off your alarm and washing your face, you set yourself in motion towards the direction of your instinct or goal, which in this case is to run early in the morning.

Again, failure to act within the first 5 seconds will give your brain the upper hand in terms of killing the instinct to go for a run. When that happens, you already lost the day even before you started it. But if you count down from 5 to 1 and launching yourself to act when you get to 1, you stack the odds against your brain and in your favor.

The Pomodoro Technique

This refers to working in 30-minute cycles of 25 straight minutes of focused work followed by a mandatory 5-minute break regardless of how fine or energetic you feel. And on every 4th work cycle, the 5-minute break is extended to 10 minutes.

What's the logic behind this? It's simple. By taking frequent short mental breaks even before mental fatigue starts to set in, you'll be able to extend your peak mental performance and consequently, personal productivity time. If you only wait until mental fatigue has set in before you take breaks, your mind (and eyes) would be too fatigued already to recover completely. When that happens, it won't be long before your mind and eyes will start to shut down and bring your personal productivity day to a close.

In contrast, taking very short but regular mental breaks even when your mind isn't tired yet extends its stamina and energy, allowing you to work longer and with greater focus too. Not only will you be able to extend your productivity hours, you'll also get to extend your high quality of focus and work.

Using the Pomodoro Technique during your deep focus work sessions isn't rocket science. All you'll need to do is to set your timer to 25 minutes and start working away until it goes off. Next, set your timer for a 5-minute break, during which you should completely disengage from whatever it is you're currently working on. The point of the break is to take one. When the alarm goes off after 5 minutes, start the next work cycle of 25-minutes work and 5-minutes mandatory break. Then on every 4th cycle, extend the break to 10 minutes.

The 25-minute work period and 5/10-minute work breaks aren't cast in stone. Feel free to experiment to see which is optimal for you. Some people use a 45-15 work-break ratio while others use a 50-10 work-break ration instead. Don't be afraid to experiment and see what works. The key here is to take short and frequent work breaks on a regular interval.

Avoiding Multi-tasking

Remember our discussion earlier about multi-tasking? In particular, about the fallacy that most people have about it, i.e., how important it is in terms of optimizing personal productivity? And more importantly, about how harmful it can actually be when it comes to personal productivity?

It shouldn't come as a surprise then that zero-multitasking is part of your time-chunking arsenal. Remember, the idea behind time-chunking is to ensure that you focus all your attention on one single task at a time so that you can create high quality work but also create it faster than if you were juggling different tasks alternately within the same time period. When you focus on just one task at a time, you enjoy the benefit of mental momentum and you won't have to restart each and every time you stop one task and starting another.

That's why it's crucial that you make it a rule for yourself to only work on one key task at a time. If you do, you get to work faster and produce consistently high-quality outputs. If you don't, you will be setting yourself up for longer work hours, higher risk of work errors, and poor-quality work. Choose between the two that you'd like to characterize your productive hours.

One of the best ways to implement the zero-multitasking protocol is to work on your most mentally challenging tasks first, especially first thing in the morning when your mind is still fresh and energetic. That way, you have more than enough willpower reserves to help you stay focused on that single biggest task for the day. Then, work on the less challenging ones so by the time your mental energy is close to being depleted, all you'll be left with are the easier tasks.

Another practical way to implement this is by going offline during your deep focus work sessions. Log off your social media and email accounts and, when possible, even from your work email or network messaging system. Just open your work email and messaging system during your lunch breaks or schedule to do them on pre-determined breaks during the day, preferably when most of your important and deep focus work has been completed. Otherwise, it'll only take one "urgent" email or work message to mentally derail you from what you'll need to accomplish at work. Remember, your work time chunk or deep focus work time should be held sacred and only emergencies should be worthy of disrupting it.

The Pareto Principle

Also referred to as the 80/20 rule or principle, it refers to a concept that renowned Italian economist who goes by the name Vilfredo Pareto popularized. He conceptualized the principle after observing that only 20% of the population during his time owned 80% of his country's land. This observation led him to study this imbalance on a deeper level and if and how it applies to other areas of life.

The Pareto principle says that 80% of the results often come from 20% of the resources, causes, effort, or factors. The Pareto Principle can be applied in a many different personal productivity aspects, e.g.:

1. Eighty percent of sales can come from only twenty percent of your prospects or customers;
2. Eighty percent of your income come from only twenty percent of your gigs or projects;
3. Eighty percent of your money-making ideas come from only twenty percent of your working hours; or
4. Eighty percent of your tasks can be done within twenty percent of the time you allot for work.

Now, the 80/20 ratio isn't an exact one. For some, 90 percent of the results may come from 30 percent of their time and effort. For some, the ratio may be 70/20. It doesn't really matter because the main point of the principle is that most of the results we achieve and want to continue achieving often comes from the smaller portion of our resources and if we want to optimally increase our results, we'd be better off focusing on those resources instead of the others that don't yield as much results.

The Pareto Principle is mostly used for managing time, especially managing personal productivity. This is because people generally have the tendency to take on too many things and spread themselves too thin, which keeps them from focusing on and accomplishing the most important tasks. If you use the Pareto Principle for time chunking, you can expect even greater results from your effort and resources.

Now, the million-dollar question is: how do you practice or apply the Pareto Principle for optimal productivity? There are several things you can do.

<u>Review Your Tasks Regularly</u>

Following the main logic of the Pareto Principle that majority of the results you get come from a small portion of your effort or resources, then you can also say that majority of your results or impact (80%) will come from a smaller portion of your tasks (20%). To apply the Pareto Principle, you should identify that top twenty percent of your tasks that will give you 80 percent of the results you're after.

When reviewing your current tasks, some of the best questions you can ask yourself that can help you identify the top twenty percent are:

1. Are the tasks in my list all classified as urgent?
2. Are the tasks in my list things I have much control or influence over or are they dependent on other people?
3. Are there specific tasks that I put so much time on?

4. Are there low-hanging tasks I can assign to others instead?
5. Are all of these tasks important for my overall goals?

Evaluate Your Goals Regularly

Oftentimes, tasks and goals are intertwined. However, it's not always the case. Some goals may not necessarily be related to your tasks. That's why it's important to regularly assess if the tasks in your list support the accomplishment of your goals. Always remember the key idea of the Pareto Principle, i.e., only a small portion of your tasks will account for majority of the results you seek. And for this, you'll need to do regular inventory of your current tasks to see which of them support your goals. For example:

1. If I put in extra hours at work today (20% of your activity), I can already finish the things I need to do tomorrow, please the department head, and be able to take an early weekend tomorrow (80% of your goals);
2. By preparing lunch at home and bringing it to work (20% activity), I can eat healthier, lose weight, and save money (80% of goals); and
3. If I focus most of my marketing time on the company's top 20 regular customers in terms of business volume (20% of resources), I will most likely increase sales coming from them (80% of the sales).

Identify Your Peak Productivity Times

Every person has that particular time of the day when productivity is at its highest. For example, some freelance writers prefer writing in the morning when they're minds are still fresh and they're able to churn out the highest number of words for the day compared to writing after lunch when they feel sluggish and sleepy. For many runners who are after mileage, they tend to have more energy when they run late in the afternoon or early evening because their bodies have had the whole day to warm up and limber. Runner who are aiming to lose weight choose to run first thing in the morning on an empty stomach because it forces their bodies to use body fat for energy, which means they get to burn more body fat and lose more weight.

Once you've identified your daily peak productivity time, schedule the twenty percent of your tasks that lead to eighty percent of the results during that time. Doing so can help you get more things done and with better quality for optimal results.

Meditation

You can optimize your time-chunking results and personal productivity through regular meditation. This ancient practice can help calm your mind en route to better focus and ultimately, personal productivity.

But what is meditation? Well, it's a state of mind where you're thinking about or focusing only on one thing, whether it's your breathing, a mantra, or silence. Regular meditation can help you achieve a state of mind that's stress-free and completely relaxed, which is conducive for optimal cognitive performance.

When your mind is relaxed, you can help activate your brain's right hemisphere, which is the creative side. When you're able to do this, you can more easily come up with new ideas to increase your personal productivity when you time-chunk. It also helps you develop your mind's ability to focus on just one thing for extended periods of time, which is key to personal productivity. Remember how multi-tasking is a personal productivity villain and how single-tasking is our hero?

Some of the benefits of regular meditation include:
1. The ability to help you recharge mentally;
2. Increased ability to focus on and remember things;

3. More mental energy for completing tasks;
4. Improved brain health and performance via increased blood flow to that area;
5. Improved planning ability;
6. Stress relief and management; and
7. Enhanced creativity.

So, how do you meditate? It's really not that complicated. One of the simplest and most practical ways to do it is through a breathing exercise called the box-breathing technique, which was popularized by bestselling author Mark Divine in his book The Way of the SEAL. Here's how to do it:

1. First, find a chair where you can sit upright comfortably with back support.
2. Sit on the chair in an upright but comfortable position.
3. Set your timer for at least 10 minutes.
4. As soon as your timer starts, put your hands on your lap, relax, close your eyes and start the breathing meditation exercise.
5. Take a slow and deep belly breath through your nose for 5 seconds. A belly breath means your stomach should be the one to expand as you take deep breaths, with minimal to no movement in your chest or shoulders.
6. Hold your breath for 5 seconds.
7. Exhale all the air through your nose for 5 seconds.
8. Hold the exhaled position for 5 seconds to complete one breath cycle.
9. Repeat the breath cycles until your timer goes off.

This is a very good meditation exercise for two reasons. First, it helps you slow down your heart rate and deepen your breath, both of which are important for keeping calm and focused. The second reason why it's one of the best meditation exercises you can do to improve focus and time chunking is because by ensuring each step of the breath cycle lasts 5 seconds, you're training your mind to focus on counting the duration of your breath cycles. If other meditation techniques use mantras, this one uses breath counts as the means by which to focus your attention.

What happens when random thoughts enter your head? No worries, just let them be and they will eventually fade for as long as you continue focusing on counting the seconds of each phase of your breath cycles. The ability to focus well isn't about being able to eliminate or eradicate random or stray thoughts. It's about being able to continue focusing on one thing in the midst of distractions. The more you practice this box-breathing technique, the stronger your focus, concentration and attention will be. Over time, you'll be able to concentrate on what you're doing even if there are distracting thoughts or things going on.

If you're new to meditation, don't be frustrated if you're not able to meditate for a minimum of ten straight minutes, if you frequently lose count of how many seconds have already passed in your current breathing cycle or if you lost track of what phase of a breathing cycle you're currently in. Meditation isn't as easy as it looks and as such, you'll need time to get used to it. The important thing is you consistently meditate – preferably first thing in the morning – because consistency creates proficiency and habit.

Conclusion

Thanks for buying this book. I hope that through this, you were able to learn a lot about how to use time-chunking to optimize your personal productivity. But more than just learning how, I hope you were also encouraged to take action and apply the things you learned here as soon as possible. You see, knowing is just half the battle for personal productivity – the other half is action or application of knowledge. Unless you apply what you learned here, you won't be able to achieve optimal personal productivity in your life.

Here's to your working smarter, getting more things done, and having more time for what matters – cheers!

How Much Of Your Life Are You In Control Of?

Do you make the most of your time, or are you always chasing your tail?

Do you make to-do lists, or are you a fly past the seat of your pants kind of guy?

Good time management allows you to accomplish more in a shorter period of time, which leads to more opportunities, lower stress and more career success.

So are you tired of setting goals and not achieve them on time? You need to learn how to fix that situation with a straightforward guide equipped with tools that help you develop and truly breathe easy.

I want to show you a unique and innovative approach to dealing with workload stress while mastering the concept of time.

I offer you a book that is proven and easy to use techniques that help you control your schedule. **And it's FREE!**

Learn how you can improve your discipline, manage procrastination and plan your work schedule.

Email us at kosvascompany@gmail.com to receive a copy of your FREE ebook.

References:

1. https://lifehacker.com/how-long-it-takes-to-get-back-on-track-after-a-distract-1720708353
2. https://melrobbins.com/blog/five-elements-5-second-rule/
3. https://www.theguardian.com/lifeandstyle/2012/jan/26/how-find-time-matters-digital
4. https://www.thebalancecareers.com/dont-multi-task-when-you-can-use-chunking-2276184
5. https://www.lifehack.org/articles/productivity/why-lists-dont-work-and-how-change-that.html
6. https://www.tonyrobbins.com/pdfs/Workbook-Time-of-your-Life.pdf
7. https://www.briantracy.com/blog/time-management/create-large-chunks-of-time-through-strategic-management-key-to-success-organizational-skills-successful-people/
8. https://www.briantracy.com/blog/leadership-success/create-large-chunks-of-time/
9. https://www.lifehacker.com.au/2014/07/productivity-101-a-primer-to-the-pomodoro-technique/
10. https://www.entrepreneur.com/article/299029
11. https://psychcentral.com/lib/10-proactive-ways-to-figure-out-whats-most-important-to-you/
12. http://fortune.com/2016/12/07/why-you-shouldnt-multitask/
13. https://www.entrepreneur.com/article/288829
14. https://michaelhyatt.com/how-to-use-batching-to-become-more-productive/
15. https://www.ntaskmanager.com/blog/best-to-do-list-apps/
16. https://timemanagementninja.com/2013/09/10-tasks-that-should-be-on-your-todo-list-today/
17. https://www.makeuseof.com/tag/time-management-rule/

18. https://www.lifehack.org/articles/productivity/how-meditation-can-help-improve-your-productivity.html
19. https://psychcentral.com/lib/10-proactive-ways-to-figure-out-whats-most-important-to-you/
20. http://fortune.com/2016/12/07/why-you-shouldnt-multitask/
21. https://www.entrepreneur.com/article/288829
22. https://michaelhyatt.com/how-to-use-batching-to-become-more-productive/
23. https://www.ntaskmanager.com/blog/best-to-do-list-apps/
24. https://timemanagementninja.com/2013/09/10-tasks-that-should-be-on-your-todo-list-today/
25. https://www.makeuseof.com/tag/time-management-rule/
26. https://www.mayoclinic.org/healthy-lifestyle/stress-management/in-depth/stress-symptoms/art-20050987
27. https://www.nimh.nih.gov/health/publications/stress/index.shtml
28. https://www.gaiam.com/blogs/discover/meditation-101-techniques-benefits-and-a-beginner-s-how-to
29. https://www.ketteringhealth.org/communityoutreach/pdf/hc/balance-work-play.pdf
30. https://gentwenty.com/work-play-balance/
31. https://thriveglobal.com/stories/7-ways-to-find-a-healthy-balance-between-work-and-play/
32. https://hbr.org/2013/01/how-to-allocate-your-time-and
33. https://www.mindtools.com/page6.html
34. http://www.skillstoolbox.com/career-and-education-skills/learning-skills/effective-learning-strategies/chunking/
35. http://www.human-memory.net/types_short.html
36. https://www.verywellmind.com/chunking-how-can-this-technique-improve-your-memory-2794969
37. https://nortonsmind.com/how-to-create-a-memory-palace-a-complete-and-thorough-manual/

www.ingramcontent.com/pod-product-compliance
Lightning Source LLC
Chambersburg PA
CBHW021834170526
45157CB00007B/2801